The Darker Side of Faery

JOHN KRUSE

GREEN MAGIC

Green Magic
Seed Factory
Aller
Langport
Somerset
TA10 0QN
England

www.greenmagicpublishing.com

Designed & typeset by Carrigboy, Wells, UK
www.carrigboy.co.uk

ISBN 9781838418571

GREEN MAGIC

Contents

CONTENTS

CONTENTS

Them and Us

Our world intersects and interacts with that of the fairies. They are constantly in proximity to us, familiar with our ways, watching our actions. What do fairies think about us? The view that has emerged in recent decades is that they are concerned to help us to heal the planet and to better ourselves, but the older tradition discloses a harder, more cynical character.

Renowned faery writer Lewis Spence remarked that "practically all supernaturals partake of human traits, more usually unpleasant ones…" Later he was blunter still: "many fairies are of a highly unpleasant character." Spence also noted Grant Stewart's 'rather unmerciful' observation that "their appetites are keen and voluptuous, as their inclinations are corrupt and wicked." Stewart went on to challenge the popular misconception that fairies are amiable and harmless people, engaged only in mirth and dancing. Rather, he said, they spend as much time thieving and blackguarding, their proneness to stealing and knavery being not the result of necessity but "the effect of wanton depravity." Stewart regarded their character, overall, as perfidious, degenerate and corrupted by passions and infirmities, by which he meant their amorous and licentious traits as well as their dishonesty, covetousness and "embezzling and criminal propensities."[1]

Grant Stewart's judgment may sound remarkably harsh, but this book will make clear that he does not exaggerate. Today

---

1 Lewis Spence, *British Fairy Origins*, 1946, 15 & 51; Grant Stewart, *Popular Superstitions*, 121–122, 103 & 109; see too J.G. Campbell, *Superstitions of the Highlands*, 32.

we might prefer to overlook it, but British folklore is very open (as well as constant) as to the undesirable characteristics of the faeries. A thievish disposition is predominant in or, even, central to their behaviour (whether this relates to chattels or to people). Other well-informed folklorists' views of faery temperament have been equally unflattering. Robert Heron called them "little beings of a doubtful character: sometimes benevolent, sometimes mischievous." Sir Walter Scott likewise characterised them as a "diminutive race of beings, of a mixed or rather dubious nature, capricious in their dispositions and mischievous in their resentment." In his *Letters on Demonology and Witchcraft,* Scott added that the elves "behaved to those who associated with them with caprice, which rendered it dangerous to displease them, and although their gifts were sometimes valuable, they were usually wantonly given and unexpectedly resumed."[2]

John Maxwell Wood, describing the faeries of Galloway and Dumfriesshire, observed that their attitude to humans generally seems to be kindly and helpful but, "underneath all their display of nobility, an elfin craftiness and capriciousness of disposition existed, malignant to a degree." Manifestations of this were their habit of striking down cattle with elf-shot and their taking of young men and women, often by means of what seem to be tragically fatal misadventures: "it was not considered good for mortals to meet with fairies face to face, however much by accident. Death might even follow such a meeting, although apparently quite natural in form."[3]

Professor John Rhys regarded the faes as thievish by nature and without equal in their larceny. Lewis Spence confirmed

---

2 Heron, *Observations Made on a Journey,* 1793, 227–228; W. Scott, *Minstrelsy of the Scottish Borders,* vol.2, VI & *Letters on Demonology,* letter IV.
3 J. Maxwell Wood, *Witchcraft & Superstitious Record in the South Western District of Scotland,* 1911, 144 & 147.

them to be "incorrigible" in their thievery. Katharine Briggs tried to explain their propensity to steal – but could not excuse it:

> "Even setting aside their thefts of human beings, mortal babies, beautiful maidens, nursing mothers and so on, there is no doubt that the fairies, like all wild creatures, felt themselves to have a right to any human possessions, particularly food."[4]

Briggs' characterisation of the faes, which seems to put them on a par with foxes and other wily predators, may again jar within our cosier inclinations, but it serves to remind us that there is a gulf of thought, as well as conduct, between our two species. For all our ability to interact sexually with fairies, they are *not* like us. They are in our world, but not wholly of it; they have a morality, but it is not informed by the religious or humane values we tend to take for granted.

John Gregorson Campbell also noted a tendency to allot ludicrous characteristics to the Highland faeries, but he explained this effort as an attempt to soften some of their more unpalatable habits in sober terms. He considered that the wish to find some mitigating humour derived partly, although not wholly, from "the recoil of the mind from the oppression of a belief in invisible beings that may be cognisant of men's affairs and only wait for an opportunity to exert an evil influence over them...".[5]

Given their pervading presence and their powers, we want to imagine faeries to be benign and well-disposed towards us. Sadly, our ancestors knew all too well that this was seldom the case.

---

4 J. Rhys, *Celtic Folklore,* vol.1, 82–83 & 251 and vol.2, 687; L. Spence, *British Fairy Tradition,* 214; K. Briggs, *Dictionary of Fairies,* 158 'Fairy Thefts.'
5 J. G. Campbell, *Superstitions of the Highlands and Islands of Scotland,* 1910, 52.

GOOD NEIGHBOURS?

The attitude of the faes to humans exposed in the folk stories may be, at best, dispassionate and can be coolly exploitative in other accounts. In fact, according to some observers, the fairies regard us with humour or even contempt.

In the anonymous 1673 text, *A Pleasant Treatise of Witches*, the author describes the fays as "little Mimick Elves" who "busy themselves chiefly in imitating the operations of men." We shouldn't mistake this for flattery though: these 'imitators of men' seem to deride us, he says – "mocking sometimes the workmen [in mines] but seldome or never hurting them."[6] This bleak view of fae conduct was repeated in an article in *Fraser's Magazine* in 1842. In *A Sketch of Scottish Diablerie in General* the writer observed that most people feel that the faeries imitate human feasts and pastimes in "fiendish mockery" and for some "hellish purpose."[7]

In this light, an isolated incident in Marjorie Johnson's *Seeing Fairies* acquires more meaning and significance. A Mrs J. Hanley recounted an experience that had occurred when she was a young woman of eighteen. Walking in the mountains near Bettws-y-coed in North Wales, she had the sensation that she was being followed and turned around. Behind her, she saw:

> "'a little man about two feet high, who looked rather as if he had been put together out of sticks or the twisty roots of gorse. He seemed too me to be swaggering along, mocking us, I think, as a small boy might so.'
>
> She turned to her companion to point out the extra-ordinary sight, but the being vanished in the moment (of course). Nevertheless, she retained the feeling that she and her friend were being watched by several unseen observers and were 'the objects of derision'."[8]

---

6 *A pleasant treatise of witches*, 1673, 53.
7 *Fraser's Magazine* vol.25, 317.
8 Johnson, *Seeing Fairies*, 2004, 24.

Why should the fairies have this attitude towards us? Scottish fairy poet James Hogg may offer part of the explanation. He was told by shepherd William Laidlaw about the latter's experiences meeting with fairies in the Ettrick Forest. Their wild unearthly eyes had –

> "turned every one upon him at the same moment and he had heard their mysterious whisperings, of which he knew no word, save now and then the repetition of his name, which was always done with a strain of pity."[9]

Perhaps this explains the fairy attitude. Humans are short-lived, they lack magical powers and they spend their time working hard to win the means to live. Compared to the carefree fae lifestyle, it must seem a comically pitiable existence, hectic with unceasing toil and prematurely ended. In this context, it's highly instructive to reread the recollections of Welsh boy Elidyr, who visited faery in the twelfth century. He recalled to Gerald of Wales that the fairy folk he had met had only contempt for humans' ambition, infidelity and inconstancy. Later Elidyr had tried to steal a golden ball from his supernatural hosts; they recovered it from him with expressions of scorn, contempt and derision. The encounters described above all appear to be modern instances of the same responses.

These accounts tend to indicate that the faery attitude to humankind is some mixture of pity and contempt. It's more complex than this, I would argue, as faery nature is darker than we would often wish to allow.

SEELIE & UNSEELIE COURTS

As stated, there is unquestionably a 'dark' side to Faery, but it is one that many contemporary commentators have chosen to

---

9 Hogg, 'Odd characters' in *Shepherd's Calendar,* 1829.

diminish or to hide. Nevertheless, some more 'Goth' fans of faerylore have kept one aspect of Scottish faerylore to the fore in their discussions: its dichotomy into 'good' and 'bad' characters. The 'seelie' and 'unseelie' courts, as they're called, are a salutary reminder of the potential negative aspects of faerydom, not least because they have come to be institutionalised and celebrated across the world.

The seelie and unseelie courts of fairies are a particular feature of the lore of Scotland's folk heritage; indeed, the clear separation of the faes into good and bad groupings that's entailed is almost unique in British, if not international, folklore. Moreover, the notion of the two courts has, in recent years, attracted considerable attention and popularity – notwithstanding the fact that they are not mentioned in the majority of the Scottish faery-lore texts and collections. Probably the majority of recorded Scottish folklore relates to the Highlands and Islands, to the Gaelic (and Norse) speaking regions, and this fact may explain why we have relatively little material documenting the two courts, which seem to be more of a Lowlands concept.

The Scots word 'seelie' derives from the Anglo-Saxon (ge)sælig/sællic meaning 'happy' or 'prosperous.' The evolution of the word in Middle English and Scots seems to have been in two directions. One sense was 'pious,' 'worthy,' 'auspicious' or 'blessed.' The second development extended the meaning incrementally through 'lucky,' 'cheerful,' 'innocent,' and 'simple,' from whence it was a short final step to 'simple-minded,' as the modern English 'silly' denotes. Because of this evolution, as well as because of the dialectical difference, it is preferable to use 'seelie' rather than try to translate it. In passing, we might observe that Scots is in many cases far nearer to original Anglo-Saxon than modern English, which has imported so many French and Latin words.

By late medieval and early modern times, 'seelie' or 'seely' in Scots meant happy or peaceable, as in 'seely wights,' and the 'seely court' was therefore the happy or pleasant court. It followed from this that 'unseelie' or 'unsilly' described something unhappy or wretched. The poet Dunbar referred to Satan's "unsall meyne" (his "wretched troop of followers") which could be a very appropriate term for the fairies; even more significantly, poet Alexander Montgomerie's description of the fairy court mentioned how "an elf on an ape an unsel begat" (that is, the pairing gave birth to a wretch or monster).[10]

Scots is the language of Lowland Scotland, and this gives us a clear sense of the realm of the seelie and unseelie courts. Accordingly, the unseelie court might, be expected to include such creatures as the red caps, shellycoat, the brown man of the muirs, the powrie, the dunter, and perhaps a hag like Gentle Annis; the seelie court, meanwhile, includes the elves who reside in Elfame, the brownies and the doonie.

Most of our records of the usage of seelie and unseelie courts are not very old. We are told about them in McPherson's *Primitive Beliefs of North East Scotland* (1929) and earlier in Charles Rogers' *Scotland, Social and Domestic* (1884); surprisingly, perhaps, there is no mention of the terms in Sir Walter Scott's *Minstrelsy of the Borders* (1802) or *Letters on Demonology* (1830) nor does Cromek allude to the concepts in his *Remains of Nithsdale Song* (1810). The ballad *Allison Gross* refers to the 'Seelie Court' but this song was only recorded in 1783 – although it might not be unreasonable to see it as being at least two hundred years older.

A very early example of the use of seelie is to be found in a poem of 1584 by Robert Sempill, entitled *Heir Followis the Legend of the Bishop of St. Androis Lyfe, Callit Mr. Patrick Adamsone, Alias Cousteane*. The poem is a biting satire upon the high-ranking churchman of St Andrews, who became a target for criticism and mockery after he used the services of a healer called Alison Pearson to treat various ailments. She was later

---

10 Dunbar, *Evergreen*, i 106.

convicted as a witch, with clear reputational repercussions for the bishop. Sempill describes at one point:

> "Ane carling of the Quene of Phareis,
> That ewill win geir to elphyne careis;
> Through all Braid Abane scho hes bene,
> On horsbak on Hallow ewin;
> And ay in seiking certayne nyghtis,
> As scho sayis, with sur sillie wychtis..."

This servant of the fairy queen is a 'carline' or 'carling' – a stout and bad-tempered woman and (by extension) a witch. She is seen riding out at Halloween across 'Albany' (Scotland) with her loyal "sillie wychtis," making it virtually certain that these 'seelie wights' are other members of the queen's court.

The word 'carling' that Sempill uses entered Northern Middle English (and Scots) from Old Norse *kerling*. The related word in southern English is 'churl' (directly from the Anglo-Saxon *ceorl* with only a minor vowel change). The hard initial consonant of 'carline' indicates the word's Norse source – and might even imply an origin in the far north, in the Viking kingdom of Orkney and Shetland.

Whilst we're debating questions of etymology, it's also useful to consider what the second element of the name, 'court,' may have implied in Scots. Certainly, it meant the royal court and could, therefore, in context refer to the establishment of the king and queen of Elphame. The word also meant a retinue, company or troop – perhaps some formal assembly of individuals as against a mere mob. Andrew Wyntoune, for example, in his *Orygynale Cronykil of Scotland* (1420) described birds and wild beasts eating carrion as a "fey court" – a 'doomed company,' perhaps.

What do these two courts do to earn their names and reputations? The 'Gude Fairies' or seelie court comprises elves whose numbers are augmented by babies who died of parental abuse, those who fell fighting in just battles and all other good and worthy folk who had, perhaps once, lapsed in some way and so could not access heaven. These good faeries help mankind: they provide bread to the poor and aged, seed corn to the hardworking, but unlucky, and gifts to those they favoured – especially those who had themselves at some point helped out the fairies with loans or gifts. If they are called on to assist a person, the seelie court will do so and will help with daily tasks. They cheer those afflicted and in despair.

The ranks of the unseelie court are made up with those who had given themselves up to the devil, bad men who died fighting, unmarried mothers stolen during childbirth and unbaptised babies. The wicked fairies are always ready to inflict harm and loss. They might shave their victims out of sheer spite, abduct people who have placed themselves in their power, steal goods and kill cattle with elf shot.

Be warned, however, that we should not overstate the benignity of even the seelie court. For example, in the *Ballad of Mary O'Craignethan*, her father curses the seelie court after his daughter is abducted by a fairy man. He threatens to cut down their groves in revenge. The father is advised how to recover his child magically but at the same time he's warned how unwise it is to make such threats. He manages to retrieve the young woman, in scenes very like the rescue of Tam Lin in the ballad of the same name,[11] but he soon dies, because "nane e'er curs'd the Seelie Court/And ever after thrave." It was well known in Scotland that conduct like that of Mary's father could only mean that the person would pine away, having seen all their affairs go to ruin. An identical fate would befall any person who ploughed up a fairy ring, as we shall see again later.[12]

In summary, then, the faerylore of Scotland explicitly reco-gnises the existence of 'bad faeries,' sorting them conveniently

11 See my *Fairy Ballads*, 2020.
12 For the 'Ballad of Mary O'Craignethan,' see *Edinburgh Magazine & Literary Miscellany*, vol.83, 1814, 527.

into one distinct body. This dichotomy is too neat, though. There are limits to the good nature of the Seelie Court, too, and when these are transgressed, the vengeance of the so-called 'good faeries' can be every bit as vicious as that of the 'bad.'

NO EARTHLY WIGHTS

Older British folklore offers us other dialect terms that may confirm the ambiguous nature of Faery and, in response, people's cautious and wary responses to the Good Folk in the past.

In the *Miller's Tale*, in Chaucer's *Canterbury Tales*, the author has a character pronounce this blessing: "I crouche thee from elves and from *wightes*." What is this strange Middle English term that appears here to be used as an equivalent to the word elves? A wight (*wicht* in Scots) can either be a human or some supernatural being – typically of the fairy family. Used to describe people like us, it will be encountered in older sources in such phrases as "living wight," "earthly wight" or "mortal wight."[13]

When applied to supernaturals, the term can encompass ghosts as well as a range of other spirits. For example, Robert of Gloucester (1260–1300) in his chronicle of English history described "a maner gostes, wiȝtes as it be" ('some sort of ghosts-wights you might say').[14] The primary meaning of the word, however, is fairies, as is clear from Richard Baxter's *The Certainty of the World of Spirits*, published in 1625: "We are not fully certain whether those Aerial Regions have not a third sort of wights that are neither Angels (Good or Fallen) nor souls of Men, and whether these called Fairies and Goblins are not such."[15]

---

13 See Spenser, *Faerie Queen*, Book III, c.III stanza 11 or Book II, c.X, stanza 70; *Description of the King of Fairy's Dress*, 1626.
14 *The Metrical Chronicle of Robert of Gloucester*, line 2750.
15 Baxter, *Certainty*, 4.

What, more than the fact that we are discussing fairies, does usage of the word by these early sources tell us? Firstly, we might remark that 'wightling' means a puppet, so that there may be some sense of a tiny stature being implied. It does *not* appear, however, that the word in itself has any sense of either good or bad. Both types of fairy can be termed 'wights'.

Scottish witch suspect Bessie Dunlop, who was tried in 1576, had an intermediary, a deceased man called Thom Reid, who was able to put her in touch with the fairies. One time he introduced her to a group of a dozen men and women whom he told her were "gude wychtis that wynnit [resided] in the Court of Elfame." Another time he showed her a group of mounted men that were "gude wichtis that wer rydand in Middil-ȝerd [Middle Earth]." A century later, the Reverend Robert Kirk, in the *Secret Commonwealth,* referred to the fairies as "subterranean wights" and "invisible wights," beings who caused a nuisance with their pranks but who were not inherently malicious, he believed.[16]

The all-encompassing and morally neutral status of the word is summarised in a traditional Scottish rhyme:

> "Gin ye ca' me imp or elf
> I rede ye look weel to yourself;
> Gin ye call me fairy
> I'll work ye muckle tarrie;
> Gind guid neibour ye ca' me
> Then guid neibour I will be;
> But gin ye ca' me seelie wicht
> I'll be your freend baith day and nicht."[17]

What's fascinating about this verse is the distinction that's made between "elf or imp," which are bad, and a "seelie wicht," a 'good

---

16   Kirk, *Secret Commonwealth,* c.12 & 'Succinct Accompt' c.8.

17   R. Chambers, *Popular Rhymes of Scotland,* 1842, 324; see too my *Fairy Ballads,* 2020.

wight.' These positive definitions are crowned by a reference in Gavin Douglas' *Aeneid* to "hevinly wightis."[18]

Frustratingly, however, this neat dichotomy proves illusory, because 'wicht' can imply a malign fairy just as much as a good one. Wicked wights are as likely to be members of the 'unseelie court' as to be benign.

We meet the seelie and unseelie court again in a lecture given by William Hay in 1564 in which he warned that:

> "there are certain women who do say that they have dealings with Diana the queen of fairies. There are others who say that the fairies are demons, and deny having any dealings with them, and say that they hold meetings with a countless multitude of simple women whom they call in our tongue 'celly vichtys' [seelie wichts]."[19]

An example of this more demonic signification of the word comes from a court case in 1661, in which a midwife from Dalkeith in Midlothian admitted that, when women were in childbed, she would place a knife under the mattress, sprinkle the bed with salt and then pray for God to "let never a worse wight waken thee...". A woman called Margaret Dickson of Pencaitland in 1643 treated a changeling child who had been taken by "evill wichts." Edinburgh woman Jonet Boyman in 1572 explained to a family that their child had died because the "sillyie wichs" had found it unsained [unblessed] one day and had therefore seized the opportunity and 'blasted' it (we'll consider faery inflicted illnesses later in the book). Lastly, Gargunnock folk healer Stein Maltman appeared before a church court in 1626 and admitted that he had told a woman how to prevent 'earthly and unearthly wights' stealing the milk from her cows. I assume the distinction

---

18 *Aeneid,* III, I, 43.
19 Hay, *Lecture on Marriage,* 1564, 127. We might, of course, call that faery queen Titania rather than Diana.

he made here was between mortal and supernatural adversaries – in other words, between witches and faery folk.[20]

The dual meaning of the term is, in fact, underlined by the Reverend Kirk, who also wrote in his book about "fearful wights" and "furious hardie wights," from whom people might protect themselves with iron. Writing around the same time as Kirk, George Sinclair in *Satan's Invisible World Discovered* made reference to prayers for protection from an "ill wight."[21]

Lastly, and underlining all these negative associations, in 1836 Robert Allan in *Evening Hours* bravely declared:

> "O, what care I for warlock wights,
> Or bogles in the glen at e'en."

All these examples demonstrate how explicitly and consistently Scottish folklore has differentiated between good and bad faeries. Whilst English and Welsh stories recognise the potential for there to be faes with bad intentions, the Scottish tales formalise and foreground that aspect of their characters. It doesn't mean that Scottish faeries are inherently worse than those living further south (although folklore in the rest of Britain struggles to find anything as undeviatingly malign as the kelpie or the *each uisge*) but the Scots decision to establish the convention of the two faery courts has given prominence and status to the darker side of faery.

In Scottish folk tales, therefore, we cannot ignore the fact that there are many unsavoury, if not repulsive and hazardous aspects to the faery character. The present book will shine the spotlight on these.

---

20 Henderson, *Scottish Fairy Belief*, 87, 97, 128 & 131.
21 Kirk, *Secret Commonwealth*, chapters 15, 12 & 4; Sinclair, *Invisible World*, 218.

SUMMARY

The view of Faery that has emerged over the last century or so is one that has them becoming ever more benign. It is the result of compounding two separate strands of thought, both of which emerged most starkly in Victorian times. On the one hand there is the perception of faes as sexy and submissive. One authority, for instance, said that the fairy was "a creature of erotic dreams and hallucinations." Victorian painters seized upon this idea as a way of smuggling portrayals of naked, alluring girls into the Royal Academy. The faery became a character in soft porn.

In the following century, the accelerating drift of faeries into the nursery, rendering them fit solely for children, deprived them of all distinguishing characteristics except sweetness. The book and postcard art of the 1920s and '30s in particular (artists such as Cicely Mary Barker, Margaret Tarrant and their many imitators) entrenched this harmless and friendly perception of the fae. In this respect, though, it's worthwhile noting that even J.M. Barrie's character Tinker Bell was very far from being an anodyne little sprite. In her original form she was a malign but curvaceous creature who was sexually jealous of Wendy's relationship with Peter Pan and sought to kill her rival.

Still, so pervasive has the amelioration of the faery character been that it makes the approach of this book seem radical and alternative, when the opposite should be the case. The experience of a millennium and a half, as enshrined in British folklore, represents the authentic statement of the nature of the faery folk of these islands. It is the pretty and sexy fairies of the last few decades that are the impostors.[22]

---

22 Spence, *British Fairy Origins*, 32, citing C.W. von Sydow, in *Folklore*, vol.45, 291.

CHAPTER ONE

Perilous Interactions. Fairy Magic in the Human World

"The fairy race is inalienably associated with magic and illusion," wrote faery authority Lewis Spence. It is inherent to our perception of them that the faes are magical beings, from which it naturally follows that, if their ability is put to malign ends, the consequences for humans can be disastrous – as well as being extremely difficult to counteract. We will consider first the nature and sources of the faeries' powers to do ill, before turning to the detailed applications of their magical abilities.[1]

FAERY MAGIC

Interestingly, Lewis Spence observed that "no difference seems to exist between that species of magic practised by fairies and that employed by mortals," other than the very significant fact that faery powers are their "natural heritage" whereas we humans must work to obtain them. In other words, if humans can be granted (or steal) magical power from the faes, they may well be able to resist them.[2]

It has been said of the faeries that they can "like those old showmen, do every kind of trick" but their magic manifests

---

1 Spence, *Fairy Tradition on Britain*, 1948, 152.
2 Spence, *Fairy Tradition on Britain*, 1948, 152.

itself in three principal forms. They can use illusion (glamour) to disguise or transform items and places; they can change their own shapes, assuming a wide range of physical forms, both animal and otherwise, and they can become invisible.[3]

In Wales, in fact, the *tylwyth teg* are so intimately associated with glamour and illusion that they denote faeryland itself. Pembrokeshire is known as a faery stronghold, as a result of which it is called *gwlad yr hud,* the land of mystery. Other epithets include *yn nhir hud a lledrith* (the land of allurement and illusion), used in Montgomeryshire, and also glossed as the 'Land of Enchantment and Glamour' in North Wales.[4]

Invisibility may be the faes' natural state, so far as humankind are concerned, but it can be brought about by wearing certain garments, by the use of fern seed, by a blow to a faery's body and by spells. In South Wales the faeries known as *Plant Rhys Ddwfn* conceal the offshore island on which they live by means of herbs growing there.[5]

In Bishop Corbet's poem *Iter Boreale,* there is an episode in which the bishop and his party are 'puck-led' near Bosworth. One of the party exclaims:

> "'Tis Robin or some spirit walks about,
> Strike him, quoth he, and it will turne to aire,
> Crosse yourselves thrice, and strike him."

The Robin in question is Robin Goodfellow, otherwise Puck, and it is fascinating to see that Christian ritual alone (even when performed by a senior cleric) will not be enough to dispel the supernatural enchantment.

---

3 Rhys *Celtic Folklore,* 168; M. de Garis, *Folklore of Guernsey,* 156: the island faeries use glamour to convert caves into grand halls, especially when midwives visit.

4 *Cardiff Times,* Dec. 26th 1874, 3: 'The Welsh Harper & the Fairies;' E. Owen, 'Folklore: Superstitions, Part 4,' *Collections Historical & Archaeological regarding Montgomeryshire,* vol.18, 1885, 144; Rhys *Celtic Folklore,* 115.

5 On fern seed, see my *Faery,* 2020, c.13; Rhys *Celtic Folklore,* 158.

As for spells of invisibility, we know that what a Highland fae would recite to hide themselves would be a charm called a *fath fithe* in Gaelic. The words of one of these are as follows:

"A magic cloud I put on thee,
From dog, from cat,
From man, from woman,
From young man, from maiden,
And from little child,
'Til I again return."

The charm concludes with an invocation of the Christian trinity and was, apparently, widely used by poachers and smugglers to hide themselves. A version of this *fath fithe* could bring down darkness to conceal the person reciting it.[6]

As we shall see later, dances in faery rings are a very common way of capturing and abducting humans. Part of the effectiveness of the rings is that, once a person has stepped inside, they become invisible thereby rendering any rescue much more difficult. Whether the human vanished because she or he holds hands with a faery during the dance, or simply steps within the magic circle of the reel, is not entirely clear, but it is very apparent that the enchantment extends to mortals.[7]

Enchanted Bread

What's worse for us, perhaps, is the fact that the faes' magical powers can take many and surprising forms. In the Scottish Highlands, for instance, the *sith* folk have a curious power over bread.

For example, on the island of Vatersay a woman was making bannocks. She heard the fairies at the door, trying to get in, but

6 MacKenzie, *Gaelic Incantations of the Hebrides*, 48.
7 Rhys, *Celtic Folklore*, 85.

she prudently ignored them. However, one of the bannocks she had just made leapt from the fire, ran to the door and opened it for the unwanted visitors. From that day hence, she always made her loaves with a hollow in the middle, which meant that they always lay still. Directly comparable is a story from the Hebridean island of Uist in which the fairies called at the door of a house for an oatcake to come out to them: the inmates threw water on the cake, and it replied: 'I can't go, I am undone.'[8]

It was widely believed that the *sith* are admitted into houses, however well-guarded otherwise, by the little hand-made cake, the last of the baking (called in Gaelic the *bonnach fallaid*) unless a hole has been made in it with the finger, a piece has been broken off, or a live coal is placed on top. The same, incidentally, can be done by the water in which men have washed their feet, by the fire, unless it has been properly raked up to keep it smouldering throughout the night, or by the band of a spinning wheel, if left stretched on the wheel.[9]

Oatmeal could also be the vector by which the *sith* folk were able to steal the substance (*toradh*) of a farmer's crops in the fields. If this is done, the appearance of a crop remains, but it is a harvest without benefit to man or beast: the ears are unfilled, the grain is without weight and the fodder lacks nourishment. There are two solutions for this. If oatmeal is carried outside at night, it's sprinkled with salt. As for the meal that's ground from the grain crop, this is also protected by salting or by a woman making a little thick oatcake with the last of the meal, which is shaped by patting between her palms (rather than kneading it like the rest of the bannocks) and by a child putting a hole through it with a forefinger. This remnant or 'palm bannock' (*bonnach boise*) should not be toasted on the griddle, but should be placed before the fire leaning against a baking stone (*leac*

---

8 *www.tobarandualchais.co.uk*, June 1960; George Henderson *Survivals of belief amongst the Celts*, 219.

9 Campbell, *Superstitions*, 19–20.

nam bonnach). This little cake with a hole in it (*bonnach beag 's toll ann*) will then counteract the faeries' magic and preserve a family's food supply. The bannocks baked should never be counted, though, otherwise the *sith* will again be enabled to steal their *toradh*.[10]

The exact nature of the faes' relationship with bread, specifically oat bread, is puzzling. They will accept loans of oatmeal from humans when they are short of flour, and the trows are known to steal oatcakes from hearths, but it is notable that it is barleymeal that tends to be returned to the lender. This preference is confirmed by a story from Highland Perthshire, in which a farmer was pestered by faery cows straying into his crops. One day, as he was yet again chasing the cattle out, a *bean sith* appeared to him and advised that if he ate barley bannocks turned on the griddle and the milk of black goats, he'd easily be able to catch the trespassing stock.[11]

What seems to be the issue here is the hardness of the bread made from the meal and its impact on the eater's physical abilities. Many of the Highland tales that illustrate this situation involve a character named Luran. In one Hebridean story a mermaid had been captured and held on land but she managed to make her escape back to the sea, calling out to Luran as he pursued her that he would have caught her if he'd eaten porridge with milk rather than dry bread. In another version from the Ardnamurchan peninsula, Luran steals a cup from a *sithean*. As he runs off the faeries make chase, one remarking "Not swift would be Luran, were it not for the hardness of his bread." In Wales there are several stories concerning attempts to lure faery women from lakes onto dry land. Bread that is neither under- nor over-baked is what tempts them. Those eating oatmeal may gain a simple physiological advantage, but given everything

---

10 Campbell, *Superstitions*, 33 & 48; MacKenzie, *Scottish Folklore*, 208.
11 Campbell, *Superstitions*, 48; E. Stewart Murray, *Scottish Gaelic Texts*, vol.7, 133, no.168.

else discussed here, it looks as though there must be a deeper magical effect.[12]

Oatcakes also have more general protective qualities, which will be described in detail in chapter five. A brief example now is the Highland custom, after three days of attending a newly delivered mother, for a departing midwife to leave behind her in front of the bed a small oatcake with a hole through it.[13]

Other Spells

Another manifestation of the faeries' magical powers is their ability to animate wood and other objects to resemble human beings. These stocks are used to disguise the abduction of adults, children and livestock. The Reverend Robert Kirk expressed the uncanny and disturbing nature of these entities well, noting how the *sith folk* possess "Pleasant Children, lyke inchanted Puppets."[14]

Worse still, as I said at the very outset, the faery world or dimension interpenetrates our own, but in a largely un-predictable and hidden manner. We cannot say with certainty when our paths may cross those of faeries, which may well indicate that constant watchfulness and preparedness is the wisest stance. Innocuous items can turn out to be enchanted, simply waiting for us to be fooled by them. For example, the bogie known as the Hedley Kow, which haunts Hedley near Ebchester, would appear as a bundle of sticks lying in the road, but if someone picked it up it would get heavier and heavier until the victim had to stop to rest – at which point the sticks became animated and bounded off laughing. Very comparable is the experience of woman from Teviotdale. A local river

---

12 M. MacPhail, 'Folklore from the Hebrides,' *Folklore,* vol.8, 1897, 384; Campbell, *Superstitions,*53; Rhys, *Celtic Folklore,* 4–6, 28 & 30.

13 Campbell, *Superstitions,* 37.

14 Kirk, *Secret Commonwealth,* c.3; Spence, *British Fairy Origins,* 40 & 42; Campbell, *Superstitions,* 83.

sprite disguised itself as a wooden beetle (a mallet), to which the woman took a fancy and carried home. During the night her window sprang open and a voice started to call her name. Fortunately for her, she instinctively blessed herself when she heard the ghostly voice – at which, the beetle became animated and flew out of the window.[15]

Knot Magic

In Ben Jonson's masque of 1610, *Oberon the Fairy Prince,* two satyrs discuss celebrations organised by Oberon. One asks if they shall "Tie about our tawny wrists/ Bracelets of the fairy twists?" Possibly related to this are some lines in Martin Lluellyn's 1646 poem *Men Miracles,* which refer to someone who "takes a silke-wormes airy twist/Such as Oberon ties about his wrist." What do these lines refer to? What on earth do they imply?

That there is some very close association between knots and magic, and between fairies and knots, is revealed by a short verse published in the *Gentleman's Magazine* for 1826. The subject of the poem is the ornate architecture of a castle, but it is clear that the author knew that the audience would understand his references to fairy lore, as irrelevant as they might initially seem:

> "Thou wouldst have thought some fairy's hand,
> Twixt poplars straight, the ozier ward
> In many a freakish knot had twin'd;
> Then framed a spell when the work was done,
> And changed the willow wreaths to stone."[16]

It seems, therefore, that knots and twists are something intimately linked to fairies. They will, of course, twist animal and human hair: as I shall discuss later the faeries like to take and ride humans and their horses at night, at the same time

---

15 Anon, *Folklore and legends: Scotland,* 1889, 171.
16 *Gentleman's Magazine,* vol.96, part 2 (New Series vol.19), 1826, 223.

tightly knotting their manes into 'pixy rings.' These knots seem to function in part as stirrups and bridles, but they also seem to be a sign of fairy control. A Perthshire man who was taken from his garden by the faeries was returned three days later with his hair all in knots – visible, physical evidence of his abduction. The knots have a practical function, therefore, but they appear to represent more than that.[17]

Scottish fairies are reported to dance around a fire at Halloween, throwing knotted blue ribbons over their left shoulders with their left hands. Those who then pick up the ribbons will fall into the fairies' power and may be abducted by them at any moment. These knots very evidently have a purely magical rather than practical purpose.[18]

In a story from Morvern in the west of Scotland, a woman and her baby from Rahoy on Loch Sunart had been kidnapped and taken into the fairy hill of Ben Iadain. She was able to appear to her husband in his dreams, telling him where she was and how to recover her. To do this, he had to go to the hill, taking the black silk handkerchief she had worn on their wedding day, with three knots tied upon it. He tied the knots in the handkerchief and, with a friend, successfully entered the hill and recovered his wife and child.[19]

The actions of twisting and binding are plainly some sort of magic spell. The ritual tying or releasing of knots is a long-established means of binding sickness to a person, or of freeing them from it. It is seen very often in folk medicine and in witchcraft and the Scottish witch trials of the seventeenth century supply several examples. What's more, many of the accused women said that they had derived their healing powers directly from the faeries, a circumstance which gives good

---

17 *Bye Gones*, Oct. 25th 1893, 205, April 10th 1895, 72 & Dec. 23rd 1896, 492; Murray, *Tales from Highland Perthshire* no.219.
18 W. Gregor, 'Stories of Fairies from Scotland,' *Folklore Journal*, vol.1, 1883, 55.
19 Campbell, *Superstitions*, 82.

grounds for suspecting that the use of knots was part and parcel of this knowledge.

Jonet Morrison of the Isle of Bute, who was tried in 1662, cured a sick baby by tying a knotted and beaded string around it for forty-eight hours, which was then removed and placed on a cat. The cat instantly died, proving that the illness had been transferred from the child to it. Jonet Murrioth, of Dunblane, was tried for witchcraft and sorcery in May 1615. She was said to have cured a patient by the simple expedient of knotting his shirt sleeve and returning it, telling him to wear the garment.[20]

What must be a closely related curing practice involved passing people through loops of yarn; the idea of release seems to be shared between the two. Janet Trall, of Blackruthen, admitted in 1623 that she had cured a man called Robert Soutar in a similar way. She passed him through a "hesp of yarn, and afterwards cut it in nine parts, and buried it in three lords' lands." Janet had learned these skills from the fairies, she said. Thomas Grieve from Fife also passed patients through yarn, in one case burning the thread afterwards. Transference and then destruction, in Trall's case supplemented by the use of magical numbers of items, are clearly ways of removing and obliterating health ill-health.[21]

There are plenty of other Scottish examples of this kind of practice. Andro Man from Aberdeen would administer cures by passing patients nine times through "ane hespe of unvatterit [undyed] yarn" and by then passing a cat nine times through in the opposite direction. Once again, the illness passed to the unfortunate cats, which promptly died. A number of Edinburgh women, tried as witches in 1597, had treated patients by passing them through garlands made of green woodbine; some did this

---

20 J. MacPhail, *Highland Papers,* vol.3, 1920, 23–27; Dalyell, *Darker Superstitions,* 520.

21 Henderson, *Scottish Fairy Belief,* 2001, 94; *Extracts from the Presbytery Book of Strathbogie,* 1843, xi; Robert Law, *Memorialls,* 1670, li fn.

three times, others nine times. One woman went through three times on three occasions twenty-four hours apart; in another instance the garland was cut up into nine pieces and burned after the ritual.[22]

Against the beneficent use of knots in cures must be placed their malign powers of protecting or cursing. These are revealed most powerfully in the account of a woman condemned as a witch at St Andrews in 1572. She faced the usual punishment for such an offence – strangling at the stake and burning –but had betrayed no fear or alarm until her jailors removed from her a white cloth "like a collore craig [a collar or neck cloth] with stringes, whair on was mony knottes." After this was taken away, she despaired. The fact that Orkney witch suspect, Isobel Haldane, had been found to have "thrie grassis bound in a knot" in her home had only added to the weight of evidence against her.[23]

Isobel Gowdie, of Auldearn near Nairn, was investigated for witchcraft in 1662. She gave a fulsome and lengthy confession that included a couple of uses of knotted threads. To steal milk from sheep and cows, she told her inquisitors that she and the other witches in her coven would take their tethers and "pull the tow and twyn it and plait it in the wrong way... and we draw the tedder (sua maid) in betwixt the cowes hinder foot and owt between the cowes forder foot and thereby take the milk." Secondly, these same witches interfered with the dyeing vats of Alexander Cummings. They took "a thread of each cullor of yairne... and did cast thrie knots on each thread... and did put the threidis in the fatt, withersones abowt in the fatt and thairby took the heall strength of the fatt away, that it could litt [dye] nothing bot onlie blak, according to the culor of the Divell."[24]

---

22 *Spalding Club Miscellany,* vol.1, part 3, 120; Pitcairn, *Ancient Criminal Trials,* vol.2(1), 25.

23 Robert Law, *Memorialls,* 1670, xxviii; *Abbotsford Club Miscellany,* vol.1, 1837, 178.

24 R. Pitcairn, *Ancient Criminal Trials of Scotland,* vol.3, part 2, 604–5.

These magical practices made their way in Scots verse as well. Alexander Montgomerie composed the *Flyting of Polwart* in the early 1580s as a ritualised mocking of Sir Patrick Hume of Polwarth. The latter was extravagantly insulted, amongst other things being accused of being born of an elf and then abandoned. His baptism proceeded in this manner, with the child being bound to Hecate:

> "Syne bare-foot and bare-leg'd to babtize that bairne
> Till a water they went be a wood side,
> They fand the shit all beshitten in his awin shearne [faeces],
> On three headed *Hecatus* to heir them they cryde
> As we haue found in the field this fundling forfairne,
> First his faith he forsakes in thee to confyde,
> Be vertue of thir words and this raw yearne,
> And whill this thrise thretty knots on this blew threed byd..."

Another satirical verse was provoked by the trial of accused witch Alison Peirsoun in 1588. She was discovered to have treated the Bishop of St Andrews and poet Robert Sempill subsequently attacked the bishop for his ungodly conduct, accusing him of "sorcerie and incantationes," amongst which were spells involving "knottis of strease [straws]."[25]

Knotted threads could inflict or transfer harm, but they could also guard against it. In the Scottish Highlands, for instance, threads called *snaithean* were used to protect children and livestock from attack by fairies or witches. Lengths of wool, coloured either red or black, would be tied around the neck or a beast's tail accompanied by a prayer and a charm that invoked aid from the trinity, Mary and various saints.[26]

---

25 Sempill, *The Legend of the Bischop of St Androis Lyfe, callit Mr Patrik Adamsoune.*"

26 A. Goodrich-Freer, 'Powers of Evil in the Outer Hebrides,' *Folklore*, vol.10, 1899, 275.

Magic Wands

As we have seen, Lewis Spence rightly remarked that "magical skill would appear to vest in the fairy race, who inherit it naturally, while mankind only acquires it." This being so, what is the purpose of the magic wand which so many fairies are reported to carry?[27]

Wands have been symbols of power for millennia. They denote civic office and since at least the twelfth century they have symbolised and conveyed magic power. In the grimoire *The Oathbound Book of Honorius*, hazel and laurel staffs are used for magical operations such as summoning demons. They are four sided with names and figures written upon them. In a fourteenth century Italian text, *The Key of Solomon*, demons are conjured and lost items are found with procedures which involve the use of wands and staffs. The former are made from hazel or other nut wood, staffs from elder, cane or rosewood. They must be of one year's growth only and must be cut with a single stroke on a propitious day at sunrise. They should be inscribed with figures on a similarly suitable day and time. The text recommends that wands should be long enough for a person to draw a circle around themselves. Later English magical texts concerned with the conjuring and binding of faeries contain very similar instructions for preparing and utilising wands.

In the ballad of the same name, the witch Allison Gross makes her magic with a conjurer's staff:

> "Then out she has taken a silver wand
> She's turned her three times round and round
> She muttered such words till my strength it did fail
> And she's turned me into an ugly worm."

---

27 Spence, *British Fairy Origins*, 17–18.

In the related ballad *The Laidly Worm and the Mackerel of the Sea*, the silver wand is used to reverse the evil spell and to turn the worm back into a gentle knight. As will be seen, in all the cases reviewed, the wand is deployed by a human seeking to wield magical powers rather than by a being who is naturally endowed with such skills.

Nevertheless, given these numerous magical associations, it was inevitable that in due course the spirits summoned should acquire their own wands. There are only a very few early examples. Scottish witch suspect John Stewart was rendered dumb and blind in one eye after the fairy king struck him with a white rod. Major Thomas Weir, whose sister communicated with the faery queen, carried a long staff which, when it touched his lips, gave him unusual energy and fluency of speech.

More recently, the imagery of wands has come to be embedded in our iconography and therefore, so it would seem, in our visions of faery kind. Marjorie Johnson's book, *Seeing Fairies*, provides a dozen examples of faeries equipped with wands. The wand is often the attribute of an individual fairy identified as a fairy queen, who will often wear a crown or coronet as well – though in one sighting in a Nottingham dentist's surgery, a group of ballet dancing fairies each waved a wand. These wands are noted as being made of silver, gold or crystal; a couple emit light; a quarter of them have stars on the end. In one case, the wand produces magic – a twist of it by the fairy queen fills a room with other dancing fairies.

Prone as witnesses are now to see wands in faeries' hands, there is scant trace of them in the older folklore. As Lewis Spence implied, it seems that the British faery is able to achieve his or her magical ends by pure thought or by gestures with the hands alone.

FAERY PROPHECY

A further magical ability of the faes, which deserves brief separate attention, is their power to see into the future. In itself, this need not be unwelcome or unfortunate, but in the majority of cases the human experience of the skill is negative.[28]

The knowledge that the faeries have of things to come may be transmitted to us in two ways. They may convey the information themselves, but is something they tend to do only obliquely, or they may use human intermediaries.

Phantom Funerals & Portents of Death

Some faery beings signify death by their very appearance to people. The *bean nighe* of the Scottish Highlands is one such, who is seen washing the shrouds of those soon to die. The *bochdan* is similar, its sighting being taken as a precursor of a sudden or violent death at the place where it's seen. In England, when a barguest or other black dog is seen, this will frequently foretell death, as with a large dog seen on the bridge at Arncliffe in North Yorkshire: it predicted the death by suicide of a man who leapt from the bridge soon afterwards. In another instance, three fresh water mermaids were seen in a pool at Blore Heath in Cheshire in 1459, singing a song that predicted the slaughter of a battle there a few days later.[29]

Sometimes, the faeries manifest a strange liking for acting out the events that are to come. For example, in 1816 a married couple were out late, completing their harvest by moonlight, at Moedin in Ceredigion. They heard the voices of a crowd passing and looked up to see a procession carrying a coffin. This was

---

28 See too my *Faery*, 2020, c.13.

29 J.G. Campbell, *Witchcraft & Second Sight*, 1902, 182; *Leeds Mercury*, June 5th 1880, 8 'Local Notes & Queries 75;' *Journal of the Chester Archaeological & Historic Society*, Part 2, 1850–51, 99; see too my *Beyond Faery*, cc.3, 9 & 10.

strange, given that it was night time, they recognised no-one and they could not understand a word that was said. The group passed by, but a little later a tailor met the same party and had to stand aside as they passed. Again, he couldn't understand a word anyone said. About three weeks later, a real funeral passed along the same route and people realised that they had seen the *tylwyth teg* acting out the event to come. Other such phantom funerals have been reported from other parts of Wales as well as from across England as well.[30]

In South Wales phantom funerals are called *y teulu anghladd* (the unburied family); in Montgomeryshire the term used is *drychiolaeth*, spectre. An account from a miner living in Llanidloes describes seeing a spectral cortege leaving the house of a very sick colleague; he himself was struck with such dread by the apparition that he was too sick to go to work for a couple of days. In another example, from Penderlwyngoch, near Gwnnws in Ceredigion, railway navvies were lodging at a farm when they witnessed a phantom funeral one evening. The sound of a group of people approaching was met with terrified barking of the farmer's dogs, after which the door opened and some pall bearers entered and apparently placed a body in the parlour – before vanishing. The navvies were very frightened, especially as there was no sign of any visitors nor any corpse. The locals knew only too well what it signified, though: the very next day one of the railway labourers was killed and his body was carried by his fellow-workmen to the farm house, just as the faeries had rehearsed the previous night.[31]

Faery predictions aren't uniformly bad, though. A faery woman who visited a cottage in Whithorn to ask for some milk for her sick child returned to the same house twenty years later. The mortal woman who had given the faery a jug of milk was at

---

30 Rhys, *Celtic Folklore*, 271–275, quoting from S. Evans, *Ysted Sioned*, 1882, 8–16.
31 E. Owen, *Welsh Folklore*, 1896, 301–302.

her door, washing tripe, and the faery said to her "You've been washing puddings these twenty years and you shall another twenty to come; you'll never want for a pickle of snuff." Both statements proved correct. In an incident from Breadalbane, a man was travelling at night to visit a mortally ill relative. Crossing a bridge, he saw a small woman wearing a green cap who was standing on the parapet. She asked where he was bound and, when he explained, she advised him that the person had already recovered – which proved to be true.[32]

'Dreaming Dreams'

The faes may also confer their prophetic skills on chosen humans. Thomas of Erceldoune, celebrated in the poem of that name, is perhaps the most famous recipient of such a gift from the faery queen, but many of the women who were accused of witchcraft and sorcery also admitted that they had received their prophetic powers from the faeries. One such was Isobell Crawford of Irvine who, at her trial in 1618, was described as "ane Pharisie" (a person with fairy powers) who could see into the future.[33]

The predictions were frequently gloomy. Jonet Andersoune of Stirling was able to predict a child's death by holding a knife over it. Isabell Haldane from Perth was carried into a faery hill in 1613 where she stayed three days. She returned home with a faery helper who told her to advise John Rioch not to bother having a new cradle made, because his expected baby would be stillborn, and who also predicted that Isabell's neighbour would die. A woman tried at Gloucester assizes in the late seventeenth century said that she was able to predict when any sick person would die or recover; she got this knowledge

---

32 Gordon Fraser, *Wigtown & Whithorn*, 1877, 355; J. Macdiarmid, 'Fragments of Breadalbane Folklore,' *Transactions of the Gaelic Society of Inverness*, vol.26, 1905, 38.

33 *The trial, confession & execution of Isobel Inch etc for witchcraft at Irvine*, 1618.

from a 'jury' of faeries who would come to her at night, their expressions revealing the patient's fate. Bessie Dunlop, from Dalry in Ayrshire, likewise had a faery adviser who gave her information about goods lost and stolen and gave prognoses on the recovery (or not) of sick individuals; for instance, in one case she was able to advise a neighbour that her child would die but that her husband would recover from an illness. Isobel Sinclair from Orkney regularly visited Elphame and there received the power of second sight, whereby "shoe will know giff thair be any fey body [doomed person] in the house." Another woman tried shortly before Isobel, called Bessie Skebister, had the same foreknowledge and was condemned for being a "dreamer of dreams." Alisoun Pearson was said to have granted, by the faeries, the power to know "what men may not know nor maidens dream."[34]

These prognostications didn't invariably involve death. Bessie Dunlop predicted a terrible fate for a young woman if she married the young man she was engaged to; her father promptly put a stop to the marriage. After sleeping with a faery man called John Stewart, Elspeth Reoch received the gift of second sight, "synding [signifying], telling and foreshawing" people what they'd done and what they would do in the time to come. Jonat Hunter, of Dundonald, in 1604 claimed to have received from the faeries the ability to "tell many things" – one of these being the identity of thieves. To end on a slightly happier note, Christiane Lewingston, of Leith, could predict the sex of unborn children: she "declarit to [Guthrie's] wyff, than being with barne, that it was a man child scho was with; as it provit in deid... all the knowledge scho had was be hir dochter, wha met with the Fairie."[35]

---

34 *Reports of the Privy Council,* 2nd series, vol.8, 346; *Extracts from the Presbytery Book of Strathboyce,* 1843, x; John Beaumont, *Treatise of Spirits,* 104–105; Dalyell, *Darker Superstitions,* 470; J. MacDonald, 'Fauns & fairies,' *Transactions of the Gaelic Society of Inverness,* vol.21, 1896, 275.

35 Pitcairn, *Ancient Criminal Trials,* vol.1, 49–58 & vol.2(1) 25; Black, *Examples*

NATURAL SITES

Knowing the danger that our 'Good Neighbours' could pose to them our ancestors were well aware of the most likely spots in the landscape to find them. These could then be shunned or, at least, approached with considerable care.

Faery rings are the site of (very rarely) faery horse racing or, most usually, dancing, a spectacle that people often yearn to watch, but they are places of danger as well as wonderment. The dances are used as a means of abducting individuals whilst the rings themselves should never be cultivated; both grazing and ploughing them are strongly discouraged. Anyone foolish enough to ignore such advice is likely to find their cattle quickly struck down with murrain, although in chapter three I shall discuss the faeries' vengeance against the farmer of Pantannas, a bitter, cross-generational vendetta that stemmed from a decision to expand cultivation by ploughing up some rings.[36]

In Welsh tradition, the perilous nature of the rings was increased by the fact that, if a person found themselves in an area marked by them, they would often find themselves trapped and unable to make an escape from the vicinity. Given the aura of magic and danger that is attached to rings, most people choose to avoid them completely: for instance, in Shropshire people went to the extreme of being reluctant to use those parts of a church graveyard marked with rings. To sleep in one is especially risky – as you may be abducted when you are both helpless and unaware. In Cornwall it was said to be dangerous for a person merely to step into a fairy ring and, if they picked a mushroom there, one of their family members would be sure to die.[37]

---

of Printed Folklore Concernign Orkney, 1903, 111; Fairies, Egyptians and Elders,' Margo Todd, in Grell & Heal, *The Impact of the European Reformation,* 2008, 193–195.

36 Rhys *Celtic Folklore,* 239 & 184; R. Chambers, *Popular Rhymes of Scotland,* 324; MacGregor, *Peat Fire Flame,* 2.

37 Rhys *Celtic Folklore,* 112; Burne, *Shropshire Folklore,* Part 1, 56; Richardson, *Table Book,* vol.2, 134; *Northern Echo,* July 12th 1894, 'Counter Spells.'

Wells are frequently fairy places where care is needed, whatever the curative properties of the waters. From lowland Scotland comes the story of a girl who sat spinning wool on a distaff by a well. When she happened to look into the water, she saw a pot of gold beneath the surface. Marking the spot with her spindle, the girl ran home to tell her father. He suspected that it was all glamour, intended to trap and drown her and, sure enough, when they returned to the place, the moor was covered in distaffs. Nonetheless, twelve men in green appeared and returned her original spindle with its wool all spun. A Welsh account from Cwm Tir Mynach, near Bala, also reveals how wells might be used as an element in the abduction of humans. A number of people had been cutting turf and one man washed his face in a well there that belonged to the *tylwyth teg*. Within a very short time he disappeared and was only found again some months later when, on the night of a full moon, he was discovered dancing in a faery ring and was, with difficulty, saved.[38]

The magical power of well water can be used against the fairies too. In the fairy-tale of the Green Lady, from Hertfordshire, a poor girl finds employment as servant to a fairy woman. One of her chores is fetching water from a well and the fish in the well warn her to neither eat the lady's food nor to spy upon her. The girl ignores the second injunction and sees the woman dancing with a bogie. She's found out and blinded, but the fairy well water restores her sight. In an East Yorkshire example of well water's magical potency, a troublesome bogle in Holderness was banished and confined in a well, since called Robin Round Cap Well. [39]

---

38 Aitken, *A Forgotten Heritage,* 18; Rhys *Celtic Folklore,* 150–151.
39 Gomme, 'The Green Lady,' *Folklore,* vol.7, 1896, 411; Nicholson, *Folklore of East Yorkshire,* 79.

FAIRY DANCES

"The tripping Fayry tricks shall play."[40]

The faeries have a malign reputation for abducting humans, both young and old. The taking of children will be examined at the end of this chapter, but here I will consider one particular way of taking grown-ups. Across Britain, a range of clever tricks are deployed for catching the unwary. For instance, the trows of Orkney and Shetland are known always to be on the look-out for attractive women to marry; one way of luring them into danger has been to put something to float on the waves near to the shore. This will catch the attention of a woman on the beach and, as soon as she steps into the sea to investigate, she risks being dragged under.[41]

Equally, it was said by one witchcraft suspect that "All sic personnes quho war tane away by suddane death went with the Phairie." This seems particularly to have been the case where a person had an accident when out riding. Around Montrose, it used to be said that a rider who died in a fall had actually been lifted and carried off by the fairies and would never be released. Interestingly, if the rider *did* manage to escape from the fairy hill and returned home, they would find themselves and their family harassed by the faes until the renegade agreed to return under the hill. I shall return to this link between faeries and the dead in chapter four.[42]

In Wales, it is known that the sudden descent of a thick mist in summer is a sign that the *tylwyth teg* are attempting to steal cattle (or children – the same trick works for both). It is also said that the best calls to round up a herd of cattle have been learned from the fairies, too; a fact that is unlikely to be unrelated.[43]

---

40 Michael Drayton, *Muse's Elysium, Eighth Nymphal.*

41 Polson, *Our Highland Folklore Heritage,* 1926, 51.

42 Trial of John Stewart, *RPC,* vol.2, 366 & 401 (1618); *www.tobarandualchais. co.uk,* Jan.13th 1979.

43 Rhys *Celtic Folklore,* vol.1, 33, 36, 91, 223 & 228; Owen, *Welsh Folklore,* 100; 'Old Summer Pastures II,' *Welsh Outlook,* vol.55, 1957, 55.

Such subterfuge notwithstanding, the fairies can be quite direct in their approaches, though. There is a story from South Ronaldsay concerning a father and daughter who were visited repeatedly by 'sea man' (possibly a kelpie). He used to enter the house at night, despite the fact that the door was barred, and would sit with the young woman until dawn. One night the father stayed up with her and made their visitor welcome. He then asked the stranger if he knew how to protect a cow against faery intrusions at night. The sea man advised cutting some hair from the beast's tail and paring its hooves. These trimmings were then to be scattered at the byre door, where they would protect the animal inside. The next night, of course, the father trimmed his daughter's hair and cut her nails and protected the house door in the manner suggested. The kelpie couldn't get in and was heard outside, cursing himself for his loose tongue. It seems pretty clear that he had been working up to a seduction and abduction of the girl, which would almost inevitably have proved fatal for her.[44]

Despite all these available strategies for entrapment and kidnapping, fairy dances are known as a very common, if not the primary, way in which mortals are enticed into fairyland and lost. We must consider why it is that humans seem to fall again and again for the trick – and what the consequences of this gullibility may be for them. As Lewis Spence perceptively remarked, "fairy dancing had a ritual complexion, and was no mere expression of elfin joyousness and vitality." We may mistake their circles dances for revels, but they have a deeper purpose.[45]

As I described in the previous section, the dances very frequently take place outdoors in so-called fairy rings, although

---

44 *www.tobarandualchais.co.uk*, Sept. 14th 1971. Dora Broome tells a related tale of the Manx *glashtyn* in her *Fairy Tales from the Isle of Man*, 1963, 40.
45 'Old Summer Pastures II,' *Welsh Outlook*, vol.55, 1957, 55; Spence, *British Fairy Origins*, 180.

other places, such as human's barns and houses, are used from time to time. The rings are themselves perilous places, but the action of dancing is far more insidiously dangerous, especially when the revelries are enhanced by the beauty of the dancing partners and the romance and mystery of moonlight. Once inside the circle, the human is likely to vanish and may never be seen again.

All reports agree that fairies are enthusiastic and talented dancers. They may not always be elegant: the trows of Orkney and Shetland are known for their love of dancing, but they limp and their dance steps are jerky and ungainly. Most faeries, though, are light on their feet and graceful and, this being the case, mortals often find themselves drawn inexorably to watch. There are several accounts from Wales indicating that a recognised community pastime was to go to see the *tylwyth teg* dancing. For example, after Sunday evening service at the church at Corwrion, near Bethesda, members of the congregation would go to a place called Pen y Boric to mingle with the fairies as they danced. The same was the case around Llanberis, Penmachno and Beddgelert, although it was acknowledged that getting too close was risky. The fact that chapel goers might be lulled into treating faery dances as social occasions indicate the subtlety of faery traps.

The peril to be guarded against was being drawn into the dancing circle. We know that fairy music in itself can be bewitching; combined with dancing in which you can also participate, it can be nigh on irresistible – and the sensation was addictive. Edward Jones of Pencwm, Llanrhystid, one night saw a fairy dance on Trichrug Hill. He described how "he felt his feet lifted up and his body light." A farmer living at Llwyn Ôn in Nant y Bettws came across the *tylwyth teg* dancing in a meadow at Cwellyn Lake. He found that:

"... little by little he was led on by the enchanting sweetness of their music and the liveliness of their playing until he had got with their circle. Soon, some kind of spell passed over him so that he lost his knowledge of the place and found himself in a country, the most beautiful he'd ever seen, where everybody spent their time in mirth and rejoicing. He had been their seven years, but it seemed but a night's dream..."

Little wonder then, that dancers can be seduced away and never return.[46]

These are the joys of elvish dancing. Given what we know about Faerie, we must expect there to be woes – and there are. In post-Reformation Scotland, fairy rings and dances acquired a particularly maleficent reputation. In Scots, the word 'gillatryp' (although it has been subject to metathesis and the vowels have been swapped around) seems to be identical to the southern English dialect word 'gallitrap,' which denotes a fairy ring, and the two terms definitely share the same supernatural connotations. 'Gallitraps' are where pixies dance and entrap humans; in Scotland, the *gillatryp* was originally the name of a witches' dance but was also used as a nickname for a suspected witch. For example, the Kirk Session of Essill in 1731 heard that "Margaret H. (*Gillatryps*) in Garmouth compeared and decleared herself penitent for her indecent practices in unseemly dances on 26th December last."[47]

A century and a half earlier, we see the word employed in its original sense. At Elgin in 1596, "Magie Tailȝeour [and] Magie Thomsoune ... confessit thame to be in ane dance callit gillatrype, singing a foull hieland sang..." It seems that the same tune or song was being played when a woman called Gelie Duncan led a diabolic procession into the church at

---

46 On faery music, see my *Faery,* 2020, c.8.
47 For discussion of 'gallitraps,' see my *British Pixies,* 2021, c.8.

North Berwick in 1589. According to Isobel Goudie in 1662, the 'maiden' or leader of the witches' coven at Auldearn was nicknamed 'Over the dyke with it' because:

> "The Devill [alwayis takis the] maiden in his hand nixt him, quhan we daunce Gillatrypes; and as they couped they would cry 'over the dyke with it."

These last examples make it very clear that the *gillatryp* was a dance with supernatural beings. What's more, whether linked to fairies or to the devil, they were ill-omened activities.[48]

As an earlier passage has already implied, the differential passage of time in Faerie and the mortal world can be one of the most serious problems for the dancer. In Aberdeenshire the association between time lost and faery company was so strong that any person delayed on a journey would be told "Ye hae surely been in Elfin."[49] Writer Lewis Spence remarked that "Years in Fairyland sometimes appear as days; the distractions of the fairy realm destroy all sense of chronological proportion."[50]

I will illustrate this, and its consequences, with a few examples of a very widely reported issue. Time may be lost to the victim, although they may not feel this to be the case and will require external evidence to prove it. A man from Haven near Pembridge in Herefordshire was lost for twenty-three years in a fairy ring – but thought it just minutes. A woman from Llangynwyd in south Wales was baking one day when she heard singing outside her cottage. She was drawn to a faery dance in the next field and, when she entered the circle, forgot her home and family entirely. She left the dance after ten minutes, to find she's been away ten years.[51]

---

48 See Joseph Wright's *English Dialect Dictionary* or George Henderson's *Folklore of the Northern Counties*, 278, footnote 2 – information supplied on Devon by Sabine Baring-Gould.

49 R. Dinnie, *An Account of the Parish of Birse*, 1865, 35.

50 Spence, *British Fairy Origins*, 52.

51 *Cardiff Times*, Sept. 25th 1909, 4: 'Welsh Tit Bits.'

A Scottish man taken into a dance under a hill was rescued a year and a day later, but he thought he was still dancing his first dance. He was only convinced of the length of his absence by seeing how his clothes had been rubbed to rags by the barrel of whisky he'd been carrying on his shoulder. In a comparable story from Bruan near Wick the man was only convinced of the duration of his absence by seeing how his baby had grown into a toddler. Likewise, a Welsh dancer was baffled how his brand-new shoes had been worn away. Two brothers from Strathspey heard fairy music from a *sithean*, a fairy hill. One wanted to enter, the other did not. The one who joined the dance was lost and his sibling was only able to rescue him a year and day later, protected by a rowan cross on his clothes. The dancer thought he'd stayed only half an hour, enough time to dance a single reel.

This loss of years from a person's life can be significant – and distressing – enough, but the impact of returning from a dance can be far worse. A Perthshire man rescued after a year and a day declared he'd only had a single dance and was not yet tired. When he got outside the fairy hill, he collapsed with exhaustion. A Welsh man who was rescued had been reduced to a mere skeleton, but immediately asked after the lost cow he'd set out to find the night (in fact, a year) before.

A Barra man disappeared whilst collecting a barrel of whisky for his wedding celebrations. After many years, a stranger appeared in his village, asking after certain people. An old man recalled the disappearance of a bride groom and had to tell the stranger that all the individuals he had mentioned were long dead. The visitor went to the local cemetery to see the graves, where he crumbled away to dust. A Shetland fiddler suffered the same fate after playing for the trows for one hundred years. A young Welsh man who was taken in a dance for seven years returned to find that his parents had both died and that his girlfriend had married someone else. His return itself didn't prove fatal, but he died of grief.[52]

If the passage of years is very long – which it often can be – the effect of a return can be disastrous. A Carmarthenshire man taken in a dance for years crumbled to dust just as soon as he stepped out of the faery ring.[53] At Cyfeiliog in Powys, a man was taken in a fairy dance in a yew forest. He was rescued a year later, but had been reduced to a skeleton. He declared he wasn't hungry but, as soon as he tasted food again, he died. In another case, being touched accidentally by a walking stick was the cause of the returnee's disintegration. For many of those who return from the dance, there is a double disappointment – of resumption of their everyday life after the heady pleasure of fairyland and, quite often, the shock of losses that have occurred whilst they have been away.[54]

As will already be apparent from these accounts, freeing yourself from a dance is no simple matter. Friends and relatives will need determination and patience to recover the lost dancer. Precise timing is essential; the rescue very often can only be affected a year and a day exactly after the disappearance and the rescuers must be protected so that they aren't also taken: iron or some other magical material will be needed to stop the fairies seizing them too or sealing them within the fairy hill. It is highly advisable for the rescuer to ensure that only one foot is put into the circle of the dance, so that some contact with non-enchanted space is retained. The fairies will resist strongly, so more than one helper may be needed to pull the victim out of the circle. The use of a magical item, such as a rowan branch, to pull the dancer out is also advisable. On such materials, see chapter five.

52 *www.tobarandualchais.co.uk,* June 1960; Jamieson, *Shetland News,* 1962–3; D. Jenkins, *Bedd Gelert,* 1899, 173. See too Campbell, *Superstitions,* 62–65.
53 W. Howells, *Cambrian Superstitions,* 1831, 141; see too *Bye Gones* October 1876, 134 & Jan.1877, 177 and Rhys, *Celtic Folklore,* 50, 155, 158 & 191.
54 *Monmouthshire Merlin,* June 9th 1854, 3: 'A Year's Sleep or a Forest of Yew Tree;' W. Howells, *Cambrian Superstitions,* 1831, 146.

Finally, in this section, we must remark upon the power of faery music. As I have described elsewhere, it is renowned for its enchanting beauty. It has been noted that "the elves are great adepts in music and dancing, and a great part of their time seems to be spent in the practice of these accomplishments... Elfin music is more melodious than human skill and instruments can produce..." Plentiful evidence confirms the captivating and unearthly quality of faery tunes. Music heard in a Welsh wood was like "numerous small silvery bells," one witness recalled; a miner from Merioneth heard the playing of "non-mortal violins" and fairies singing in a garden at Bettws-Cedewain produced the "most delightful music" the listener had ever heard. These qualities are simultaneously the danger of faery music. At Pantybeudy, near Nantcwnlle in Ceredigion, there used to be numerous faery rings to be seen in the fields and meadows during late Victorian times. Beautiful faery singing was heard there on moonlit nights and people were drawn to the rings to listen. However, if anyone got too near, it was known that the *tylwyth teg* would take them forever.[55]

GLAMOUR HOUSES

A faery trick somewhat related to the traps laid by faery rings, and a prime example of the faery deployment of magical illusion on a grand scale, is the curious phenomenon of what I term 'glamour houses,' the faery-created illusion of buildings offering shelter and entertainment to humans that don't actually exist.

A man was lost in the dark in deep snow on top of the Cotswold Hills near Dursley in Gloucestershire. Unexpectedly, and to his relief, he came across an inn where he found a room for the night. He slept well and found an excellent breakfast

55 Campbell, *Superstitions*, 18 & 153; *Bye Gones*, Dec. 12th 1891, July 17th 1889, 171 & Sept. 29th, 1897, 209; see my *Faery*, 2020, c.8.

laid out for him the next morning. When he was ready to leave, he couldn't find any staff around, so he placed two guineas in payment for his accommodation on the counter before continuing his journey. Arriving at his destination, he told his friends of his good fortune the previous night, but they said there was no such inn in the place he described. Returning to the spot to settle the argument, the traveller found no sign of the tavern, but his coins were still there, lying in the snow.[56]

The Phenomenon

The 'glamour house' phenomenon seems to be a particular feature of the fairies of Wales and the borders of England. The vast majority of the examples come from North Wales. Thomas Hardy even made use of the idea in a late poem, *The Paphian Ball,* in which a church band comes across a large house none of them knows. They are asked to play dance music for the assembled company, but late in the evening they start to play a carol (it being Christmas) – the effect of which is to make everything around them vanish, leaving the band out on the empty heath.

All of the reported incidents took place at night; in several, the human was lost in bad weather. In a couple of examples, the traveller is a farmer returning from a fair (one at Pwllheli in Lleyn; the other at Beddgelert near Snowdon). This fact may, of course, make us suspicious that each had been drinking after a good day buying and selling. The same might be said of a man called Ianto, who was returning home very late after a wedding. The rest of the cases don't give grounds for such doubts, though. A shepherd from Cwm Llan, near Beddgelert, went out onto the mountain to search of his flock and got lost in mist; a harpist setting out from his home at Ysbyty Ifan to walk to Bala was also caught by mist and lost his way so that he fell in a bog;

---

56 Briggs, *Folklore of the Cotswolds,* 1974, 81.

people returning home after peeling rushes at Llithfaen, near Llanaelhaearn on Lleyn, came across a fairy dance.[57]

However, it may be that they find themselves far from home in the dark, the usual experience of the 'glamour house' is to be invited in, either to receive shelter or even to join in festivities, whether that may be a wedding celebration or simply communal singing and dancing. The traveller is made welcome, fed, warmed and, eventually, given a comfortable bed for the night, in which they sleep well after their wandering and the good company they've enjoyed. The sequel is always the same: they awake next morning to find the house or tavern vanished. The man returning from Pwllheli awoke on a pile of ashes; more commonly, the man finds himself lying on heather or rushes, perhaps with a clump of moss for his pillow. The Bala harpist found himself in a sheepfold, with his dog licking his face. Ianto had the luckiest escape, for after being 'pixy-led' by music through bogs and thickets, he awoke not in a fine house but on the very edge of a precipice.[58]

To conclude this introduction, I'll mention two out-lying cases, which indicate that the 'glamour house' phenomenon is part of a more general faery tendency to disguise their identities and to delude humans. The first example comes from the Simonside Hills in Northumberland. A traveller was wandering upon the moorland at Simonside at night when he saw a faint light ahead and found a little hut containing the embers of a fire, two rough grey stones and two old wooden gate-posts. He sat down on one of the stones and was adding some brush wood to the fire when a small human shaped figure, no higher than his knee, came waddling in and sat down facing him on the other stone. The traveller remained silent so not to annoy the creature, who was a *duergar* or dwarf, but he began to feel the cold again and so snapped a length of wood over his knee, placing the pieces

57 D. Jenkins, *Bedd Gelert*, 1899, 129.
58 Rhys, *Celtic Folklore*, vol.1, 99, 115, 150, 203 & 208.

on the fire. The strange intruder seemed angered by this and picked up one of the gate posts, which he likewise broke over his knee and added it to the fire. The traveller, wary of irritating his companion further, permitted the fire to die away and remained silent. It was not until dawn the following day, when the dwarf and his hut had both disappeared, that the traveller realised the true extent of the danger he'd been in. He found himself still sat upon the grey stone, but on the edge of a deep precipice, over which he could have easily fallen to his death with a single movement.[59]

Our second example comes from the north of Scotland. Andro Man, an Aberdeen man tried for sorcery in 1598, described to his accusers how "the elphs" would make it appear like he was in a fine chamber but he would find that he was really in a moss (a bog) on the moor. They seemed to have candles and lights and swords, but it was nothing but grass and straws, he said ruefully. The commonest examples of this use of glamour are to be found in the stories of midwives taken to fairy homes to attend a woman in labour. The midwife is asked to anoint the new baby with an ointment and told that she must not touch her eyes with the same salve, but of course this happens and, when it does, she obtains the second sight and sees through the glamour cast about her. Usually, as in the Welsh story of Eilian of Garth Dorwen, she sees that what she supposed to be a handsome mansion is in fact just a damp and miserable cave or hovel. Sometimes, as in the Cornish story of *The Nurse Who Broke Her Promise* by Enys Tregarthen, the reverse is the case and a rough hut turns out to be a palace.[60]

---

59 See F. Grice, *Folk Tales of the North Country,* 1944, c.38 or Tibbit, *English Fairy Tales,* 1902.

60 *Spalding Club Miscellany,* volume 1, part 3, 121; Briggs, *Dictionary,* 'Fairy Midwives;' Tregarthen, 1940.

Key Features

To summarise these experiences, then, people are out wandering very late at night; they may be lost or they may be in danger from fog or a blizzard. They are given somewhere warm to sleep and, generally, awake outside under blue skies the next day. The Dursley story is slightly different in that the illusion persists well into the next day, until the man has ridden off to meet his friends in Stroud. The only major departure from this pattern is an account from Llyn Bwch in the north of Ynys Mon (Anglesey). Here young people would regularly go out on moonlit nights to see the fairies celebrating. They would find a grand palace standing where none existed during the day time and would see the fairies there, dancing and enjoying themselves. In the mornings afterwards, the palace would have vanished but fairy rings might be seen and fairy money might often be found.

Motivations

Who do the fairies do this? To begin with, it's worth reminding ourselves that the fairies are perfectly capable if they wish of building such structures in reality – whether for themselves or for human customers.[61]

Secondly, their magical powers are such that they can easily construct the simulacrum of a house, inn or palace that appears to a visitor to be physical and real but yet is nothing but glamour. A good example of this comes from the ballad of the *Wee Wee Man*. The narrator of the song meets the fairy of the title when he is out walking. He is invited to visit the fairy's 'bonny bower' which stands on a nearby green:

> "… we cam to a bonny ha';
> The roof was o' the beaten gowd,
> The flure was o' the crystal a'.

---

61 See my *Faery*, 2020, c.7 or *How Things Work in Faery*, 2021, 124.

When we cam there, wi' wee wee knichts
War ladies dancing, jimp and sma',
But in the twinkling of an eie,
Baith green and ha' war clein awa'."

The Wee Wee Man creates the illusion of a splendid hall, built of sumptuous materials, but it can vanish in an instant. This exactly what we see in these stories of transitory inns.

We might say that this is an excellent way to lure humans into your clutches and, as such, is an elaborate form of pixy-leading. Indeed, it is true, that Ianto ended up in the fine house where he slept after vainly following fairy music and voices for miles in the dark. There is some mischief involved, but very little, and no-one is ever harmed or abducted in these incidents.

On the whole, therefore, deliberate deception does not seem to be the aim. Whilst it's correct to observe that none of the splendid rooms the people see, the luxurious beds in which they sleep, the food they eat or the pleasant people they meet are really there, or are what they seem, the aim nonetheless appears to be to help or even protect a lost traveller. At the very least they are given free entertainment and food. All of this may seem to be a strange and elaborate way of behaving, but the fairies can be extravagant with their favourites. The practice is, in this way, related to the habit of the fairies to adopt favoured humans and to grant them money – in light of which it's interesting to note that the lost shepherd from Cwm Llan found silver coins in his shoes when he awoke and, weekly for a long time after that, he would find a coin between two stones at the spot where he had slept (until he told someone about his luck, of course).

SPELLS FOR SUMMONING THE FAE

There are plenty of people who wish to have face to face contact with faeries, whether that's just to dance with them or because the individual wishes to develop some longer lasting relationship, be that one of master and servant, using the faery's supernatural knowledge to their advantage, or a sexual liaison (a number of spells for acquiring faery lovers have been preserved).[62]

Broadly, there seem to be two ways in which it is possible to summon fairies into your presence. One involves the use of wands, a crystal ball and the conjuring of the faery with the correct words; the other exploits the faeries' own magic or glamour to override their invisibility and expose them to our view.

The first method was the one adopted by many magicians and seers, especially during the sixteenth and seventeenth centuries, when efforts to contact spirits by these means seem to have been at their peak. One of the leading English practitioners was William Lilly, who described some of the methods used in his *History of His Life and Times*. He tells us that he knew two skilled seers. One was a woman called Sara Skelhorn who practiced in the Gray's Inn Road in London. She contacted beings she described as angels through her crystal ball and gained information from them. In fact, Sara seems to have been rather too good at this. Late in her life, she complained to Lilly how the angels wouldn't go away, but followed her around her house until she was weary of their presence.

The other conjurer Lilly knew was a woman called Ellen Evans, who summoned up the fairy queen using her crystal ball and a summoning spell, that began *"O Micol! O Micol! Regina pigmeorum veni..."* (Micol, come, queen of the pygmies [fairies]). This line is evidently the start of a much longer invocation.

At this point Lilly went on to warn his readers that the spirits won't appear for everyone. They prefer people of "strict diet and upright life." Moreover, even if they do appear, it will often

---

62 See my *Love & Sex in Faeryland,* 2021.

transpire that the magician is not suited to the experience. As Lilly says, even those of undaunted character and firm resolution can be astonished and trembling "nor can many endure their glorious aspects." However much you may desire to see the faery queen, therefore, the reality may be overwhelming; her power and beauty may be enticing, but humans frequently are no match for a fae, either physically or in magical terms. The would-be magician may be incapacitated by fear in the presence of the faery queen: at least one of the spells for summoning a faery lover hints that the male conjurer may find his partner rather intimidating. The supernatural is brought forth for "bountiful copulation" but, once she's laid on the magus' bed, he's counselled to do "with her whatsoever you please – *or canst do...*"

The second way to see fairies is to use their own magic against them. A seventeenth century spell book in the Bodleian library in Oxford contains a variety of faery-related spells, including one titled 'To call Oberon into a crystal stone' which is clearly an attempt to subdue the faery king to the operator's will. Here, however, I wish to discuss a slightly more modest spell, called '*Experimentum optimum verrisimum* for the fairies.' It sets out a rather lengthy and complex procedure, which I reproduce here:

"In the night before the newe móone, or the same night, or the night after the newe moone, or els the night before the full moone, the night of the full, or the night after the full moone, goe to the house where the fairies mayds doe use and provide you a fayre and cleane buckett, or payle cleane washt, with cleere water therein and sett yt by the chimney syde or where fyre is made, and having a fayre newe towel or one cleane washt by, and so departe till the morning; then be thou the first that shall come to the buckett or water before the sonne ryse, and take yt to the light, that you find upon the water a whyte ryme, like rawe milk or grease, take yt by with a silver spoone, and put yt into a cleane sawcer; then the next night following come to the same house agayne before 11 of the clocke at night, making a good fire with sweet woods and sett upon the table a newe towel or one cleane washt and upon yt 3 fyne loaves of new mangett [fine wheat bread], 3 newe knyves with whyte haftes and a newe cuppe fulle of newe ale, then sett your selfe downe by the fyre in a chaire with your face towards the table and anonynt your eyes with the same creame or oyle aforesaid. Then you shall see come by you thre fayre maydes, and as they passe by they will obey you with becking their heads to you, and like as they doe to you, so doe you to them, but saye nothing. Suffer the first, whatsoever she be, to passe, for she is malignant, but to the second or third as you like best reach forth your hand and pluck her to you, and with fewe words aske her when she will apoynt a place to meete you the next morning for to assoyle such questions as you will demand of her; and then, yf she will graunt you, suffer her to depart and goe to her companye till the houre appointed, but misse her not at the tyme and place; then will the other, in the mean tyme whyle you are talking with her, goe to the table and eat of that ys ther, then will they depart from you, and as they obey you, doe you the like to them saying nothinge, but letting them depart quyetlye. Then when youre houre is come to meete, say to her your mynde, for then will she come alone. Then covenant with her for all matters convenient for your purpose and she wilbe always with you, of this assure yourselfe for it is proved, ffinis [the end]."

The process is reasonably straightforward, as you will have seen. You will need to have acquired some fresh fine loaves, some new ale, some clean buckets filled with clean water and some clean towels, but none of these items ought to be too hard to come by. The tricky part is knowing whether a house is one "where the fairies mayds doe use," in other words, a place that is frequented by female fairies on a regular basis. Provided that you're sure you've correctly identified the place, and provided that the time is right, everything else will apparently fall into place like clockwork.

How does this ritual work? Well, as fairy expert Katharine Briggs explains, the unspoken assumption lying behind it is as follows: overnight the fairies will enter the house to wash themselves and their children in the fresh water. Fairy babies are anointed with an ointment that gives them their second sight and powers of glamour and (it seems) reinforces their immortal fairy nature. Some of this will, it seems, be washed off during the ablutions and it is this that forms the rime on the surface of the bucket. You then simply lift it off with your silver spoon and you have acquired the key to faery. It is not so much about constraining a fae as revealing one that was there already, but concealed by glamour.

Lastly, it is worthwhile underlining the potential risks of the processes described. Bringing a faery to you against her will – and then attempting to subdue and control her – were activities fraught with peril, which the recorded spells readily acknowledge. One spell required that the faery assist the conjuror "without anie deceipt or tarrieng; nor yet that thou shalt have anie power of my bodie or soule, earthlie or ghostlie, nor yet to perish so much of my bodie as one haire of my head." Another demands the faery's aid "without fraud or harm or illusion or bodily wound." A third warns the conjured spirit that "No power or powers thee shall have of my body earthly to do me harm, neither sleeping nor waking, neither yet to hurt any other creatures or other things in the whole world." John Beaumont had the second sight and constantly saw faery men and women surrounding him; he readily admitted that he often felt scared and, as often, dismayed by the faeries' want of morals – for they were promiscuous and spoke "loosely" (in vulgar terms). As we read earlier, both William Lilly and his mediums confessed to being shocked and shaken in the faery presence.[63]

Despite the authors' obsession with material gain – whether that was discovering hidden treasure or just possession of a supernatural being for sex – they did not endeavour to disguise the hazards involved

ACQUIRING AND LOSING FAIRY SECOND SIGHT

As we have just seen, acquisition of the second sight, and the ability to see through fairy glamour and watch the activities of the Good Folk, is a gift that many desire. It has to be said, though, that the spells just described seem to be a very laborious way of acquiring the sight, as it can come from many sources, some easily achieved (it would appear); many purely fortuitous.

Let's start with the cases of luck. Gaining second sight could depend upon nothing more than the time of your birth. A Lincolnshire woman told one folklorist that she had been born at twilight and could see things that other people couldn't. However, it also meant that she hesitated to go out at twilight, because she often saw things that terrified her. Being in the right place, at the right time, might also be significant. In one Scottish case, a child left asleep upon a fairy knoll came away from the spot endowed with the second sight. Whether this was a matter of the place alone, or the result of an intervention by the *sith* folk because they had chosen to favour the infant, we cannot tell.[64]

---

63 R. Scot, *Discoverie of Witchcraft*, 1584, Book 13, c.8; British Library, Sloane 3850, ff.145–166; Folger Library, MS Xd 234; Beaumont, *Treatise of Spirits*, 1705, 91–93 & 394–396; Lilly, *History of His Life & Times*, 1715, 228.
64 *Lincolnshire Notes and Queries*, vol.2, 1891, 144.

It seems that the second sight may also be obtained through faery food. Cromek recorded that a person invited inside a fairy hill to feast with the inhabitants went away afterwards with the second sight, implying that consuming the food itself – or perhaps the proximity to the fairies during the meal – could have been the source. If it was the food, this will of course be in stark contrast to the usual outcome, in which the person eating faery food in Faery becomes trapped there. Another example of this same process comes from Skye – and significantly takes place on human terrain rather than inside a faery hill. Two men were out peat cutting. One paused and wished for a drink of milk, in response to which a faery women appeared and gave him exactly what he hoped for. He drank gratefully, but his friend refused for fear of faery influence. The one who had partaken found that he could see a host of faeries throwing darts at his companion. Conversely, food products less favourable to the *sith* folk may inhibit our ability to see them. Hence, on the island of Skye, it was believed that as oats were not a proper food for the faeries, any person who wished to be able to see them should not have oats about themselves when they went out in the hope of encountering them – although normally carrying oats was recommended as a protective measure for travellers.[65]

Close physical contact with the fairies seems to be fundamental to many transfers, as is seen in Enys Tregarthen's 1940 story of the fairy child Skerry Werry. A lost fairy child was taken in and cared for by a widow on Bodmin Moor. The longer the little girl stayed, the better the old woman's 'pixy sight' became, so that she could see the pisky lights on the moor. This account implies that it was simply Skerry-Werry's residence that had the magical effect. More traditionally, as in Tregarthen's story of the same year, *The Nurse Who Broke Her Promise*, a human midwife bathing a fairy baby is told not to

65 J. Maxwell Wood, *Witchcraft & Superstitious Record*, 180; Seton Gordon, *The Charm of Skye*, 1929, 232; Campbell, *Superstitions*, 48.

splash bath water in her eyes (or, even more commonly is asked to anoint the child with ointment, but not touch herself) and a breach of such an injunction is what transfers the magic vision. Of course, although Tregarthen doesn't report this explicitly, we can probably assume that whilst Skerry Werry was living with the old woman she would have bathed the little girl and might therefore have splashed bath water into her eyes...

A third example of transfer by bodily contact is even stranger: an old Somerset woman who used to nurse those who were sick was one day walking to a well for water when a moth brushed against her face. This gave her the pixy-sight and she immediately saw a little man, who asked her to go with him immediately to tend his seriously ill wife.[66]

Then again, close association with faerie kind on a regular and prolonged basis can certainly convey second sight. As we saw a little earlier, Orkney woman Isobel Sinclair at her trial in 1633 confessed that, over a period of seven years, she had at the quarter times of the year "bein controlled with the Phairie, and that be thame, shoe hath the second sight..."[67]

It also seems that items used or worn by the faeries might convey second sight to a human if she or he takes possession of them. A man called John MacDonald fought a kelpie, using a cudgel. One of his blows broke the water horse's bridle, which fell off. John snatched it up and instantly the kelpie was at his mercy. John also discovered that, if he looked through the holes in the bit, he could see hosts of fairies and witches, all of whom would do his bidding.[68]

Gifts of second sight from the fairies are certainly reported: rarely ointment or 'dew' might be applied by the faery to the human's eyes, more often the person might be told how to

---

66 Mathews, *Tales of the Blackdown Borderland,* 59.
67 Dalyell, *Darker Superstitions,* 470.
68 Polson, *Our Highland Folklore Heritage,* 1926, 82.

acquire the sight.[69] Elspeth Reoch was tried in 1618 and confessed that she had had contact with the faeries and they had given her ability to see into the future and tell fortunes. Elspeth had been instructed in two methods of obtaining the second sight. One was to roast an egg on three successive Sundays and to use the 'sweat of it' (the moisture that appeared on the shell, presumably) to wash her hands and then rub her eyes. The second technique was to pick the flower called millefleur and, kneeling on her right knee, to pull the plant between her middle finger and thumb, invoking the Christian trinity. The grease of a roasted goose was prescribed to another man for this same purpose.[70]

Once one person has the gift, others can benefit from it. Contact with the gifted individual, either by touching them or by looking over a shoulder, will reveal the fairies to the second person as well. Be warned, though. The fairies object to uninvited intrusions and to any behaviour they regard as spying. There is a Victorian report of a case from Wrexham in which a fairy blinded a person just because he looked at it. A very similar account comes from Exmoor: a person who 'had dealings' with the pixies later saw them thieving at the market in Minehead. When she protested, she was blinded. Alone, these cases might appear to be truncated versions of the midwife stories mentioned earlier; these nearly always culminate with the midwife spotting the fairy father on a later occasion, whether he is stealing goods at a fair or market or simply out and about in the human world. She addresses him, giving away her secret, and, in response, she is blinded, whether by a breath in the face or some more physical means. However, the Wrexham and Minehead stories both suggest that anyone who has the second sight, for whatever reason, might suffer as a consequence if a fairy objects to it.[71]

---

69 J. Maxwell Wood, *Witchcraft & Superstitious Record*, 178.
70 *Maitland Miscellany*, vol.2, part 1, 187–191; see too W. Scott, *Minstrelsy*, V.
71 *Bye Gones*, series 1, vol.3, 1876–77, 149; Palmer, *Folklore of Somerset*, 22.

Seeing through the fairies' glamour risks exposing those aspects of their conduct that they might rather keep concealed from us (their propensity for stealing our property perhaps being the least of them). Knowing their secrets can put us in peril, so that it is possibly rash to wish too fervently for knowledge of their hidden world.

TAKEN BY THE *SLUAGH*

The *sluagh*, or fairy host, is well-known in the Highlands of Scotland for carrying off people so as to use them for a variety of more or less malign purposes. The host is known by several names in Gaelic, all of which give us some clue as to their nature or origin. Lewis Spence referred to them as the *sluagh eotrom* (or *eutram),* meaning the 'light' or the 'aery' host. This may reflect their flight through the air, or even their physical nature. The Reverend Kirk, meanwhile, distinguished between the *sluagh saoghalta* and the *sluagh sith*. The latter is the 'fairy host' and the former the 'secular' or 'worldly' host. If we understand that 'sluagh' more broadly denotes people or population, this makes sense of what Kirk says next: "Souls goe to the *Sith* when dislodged." In other words, once mortal people die, they leave their earthly communities and join the fairy host instead. Thus, on the Hebrides, the bier used to carry a corpse to burial would then be smashed against a special tree, deliberately to stop the *sluagh* using it later to carry away the dead person.[72]

Going with the Host

We can learn something more about the *sluagh's* nature from actual experiences of contact with the host. John MacPhee of Uist was outside his house one night when he heard a noise coming from the west (a notoriously fay compass bearing)

---

72 Spence, *British Fairy Tradition,* 60; Kirk, *Secret Commonwealth,* 'Succinct Accompt,' 9 (10); E. Hull, *Folklore of the British Isles,* 245.

which sounded like the breaking of the sea. MacPhee saw a mass of small men coming in a crowd from that direction and suddenly felt hot, as if a crowd of people had surrounded him and were pressing in, breathing upon him. Then he was carried off at great speed, flying through the air to the graveyard at Dalibrog, seventeen miles distant. For a moment or two he was set down and the sensation of heat left him. Then the host returned, he felt hot again, and was carried back to his home. After this experience, MacPhee became sickly and thin, suffering what are some of the typical physical effects of fairy contact. Although the author of the account refers to the host as 'the dead,' their living physicality seems very much to contradict this description. The same is true perhaps for those people who are taken repeatedly by the *sluagh*. Mistreatment by the host can be a common experience, with victims being 'rolled, dragged and trounced in mud and mire and pools.' This can leave the victims pale, awe-stuck, terrorised and in extreme exhaustion and such flights often prove fatal.[73]

If a person is called to travel with the *sluagh*, there is no denying the summons; this is called 'going with the host' (*falbh air an t-sluagh*). In another instance, a man on Skye saw the host approaching and begged his companion to hold him tightly to prevent his abduction. Despite the friend's best efforts, the victim began to 'hop and dance' before rising off the ground and being carried a couple of miles. In a second instance, we know of one man on Uist who was taken by the *sluagh* every night, being transported to many of the Hebridean islands. He knew when they would come and that he would have no choice to go with them, leaving immediately they arrived. It's been said too that a dismal sound precedes the host, which perhaps its victims learn to detect.[74]

---

73 Campbell & Hall, *Strange Things*, 267 no.37 & 297, no.52; Watson, 'Celtic Mythology,' *Celtic Review*, vol.5, 1908–9, 60.

74 *www.tobaranualchais.co.uk*, 1959; Campbell, *Popular Tales*, vol.4, 340; J. Campbell, *Strange Things*, 2006, 267 no.37.

How the Host Flies

The mass nature of the *sluagh* is apparent. They travel in a multitude – according to one Scottish witness "in great clouds, up and down the face of the world like starlings." As will be seen from subsequent testimonies, comparisons to flocks of birds or beasts are common. On Barra, Evans Wentz was told that the host went about at midnight, travelling in fine weather against the wind like a covey of birds.[75]

The host travels across the land by several means. They very frequently use whirlwinds, as Scottish witch suspect, Bessie Dunlop, attested. She had been visited by twelve fairy folk who left her in "ane hideous uglie sowche of wind." A *sowche* is a sough, a rushing or whistling. In the Highlands it's believed that, when 'the folk' move about in groups, they travel in eddies of wind which are known as `the people's puff of wind' (*oiteag sluaigh*). Suspected witch Barbara Parish of Livingstone told her trial in May 1647 that the Good Neighbours she met went from place to place in this manner; in 1661 Bessie Flinkar of Libberton gave a similar account to her accusers. These are examples from Scottish popular belief; the notion was certainly in circulation in literary culture (at the very least) well before the mid-seventeenth century, as the late-fifteenth century verse, *The Crying of Ane Playe,* illustrates. Harry Hobbilschowe claims to have come from fairyland, in Syria, "with the quhorle wind."[76]

As we shall see, this spinning air can act partly as a cover for human abductions, as a form of concealment *and* as a means of inflicting harm on people. An immediate example is the band of Highland fairies called 'Friday's People' (*Muintirr Fhionlaidh*) who travel on calm days in whirlwinds, occasionally picking up those found asleep en route and carrying them a short distance.[77]

---

75 Watson, 'Celtic Mythology,' *Celtic Review,* vol.5, 1908–9, 59; Evans Wentz, *Fairy Faith,* 108; Carmichael, *Carmina Gadelica,* vol.2, 308.
76 MacPhail, 'Fairylore from the Hebrides,' *Folklore,* vol.7, 1896, 402.
77 *Folklore* vol.16, 177 & vol.7, 402.

What's more, this mode of conveyance isn't restricted to the Highland host: It seems to be used throughout the Britain Isles, from the Forest of Dean all the way north to Lewis in the Scottish Outer Hebrides. For example, as far away as Jersey the *faitiaux* travel around in whirlwinds, carrying off people and animals. It's said there that a person can be rescued from the eddy by throwing something into it – a left shoe, a bonnet, a knife. horse dung or earth from a mole hill (throughout Britain, in fact, churchyard or mole hill earth have similar magical properties against the faes).[78]

The *sluagh* can also travel on objects imbued with faery glamour, such as bulrushes, docks, ragwort and withered grass stems, so that one description of their motion is 'travelling on tall grass stems' (*falbh air chuiseagan treorach*). Humans who have witnessed this have been able to imitate the fairies' actions and transfer their magic power to other items on which to fly, such as ploughs or loom beams. In truth, physical travel is not necessary at all, for a man in Sutherland was taken in spirit one night by the *sluagh*, even after his friends had forcibly restrained his body to try to prevent his abduction.[79]

Why the Host Flies

The reason for these journeys seems to be uniformly malicious. The primary aim is to abduct humans, and secondary purposes are shooting elf-bolts at people and livestock or stealing human property – usually food and drink.[80] People may be carried a short distance of just a few miles, or they may be carried away over the ocean to other islands or even different countries. For example, some trows flew all the way from Shetland to Norway

78 John L'Amy, *Jersey Folklore*, 1927, 24; Campbell, *Superstitions*, 26.
79 Mackay, 'Fairies in Sutherland,' *Celtic Magazine*, vol.9, 1884, 207; Aubrey, *Miscellanies*, 149; Monteath, *Dunblane Traditions*, 101; Pitcairn, *Ancient Criminal Trials*, vol.3, part 2, 608.
80 Monteath, *Dunblane Traditions*, 101.

to abduct a newly married woman, and some fairies in Moray conveyed a man to Paris, although much more local journeys are more typical. Sometimes a person picked up by the *sluagh* will simply disappear for a while; on other occasions, they may appear to die to their friends and family whilst their living body is carried off by the host.[81]

Flight may also be used as a punishment against one who's offended or annoyed the *sith*. A Perthshire herdsman who had prevented the fairies carrying off a new-born child and its mother was promptly carried off through the air for six or seven miles and back again before being unceremoniously dropped down through the smoke hole of his father's cottage. In just the same way, a minister in Ross-shire had spoken slightingly of the fairies and they exacted their revenge by picking him up and carrying him head over heels through the air. Here the aerial abductions are plainly acts of revenge for thwarting the fairies' wills or disrespecting them.[82]

Similar stories of aerial abduction come from Wales, too, and from them we learn that this form of flight is not necessarily pleasant for the human taken along. The Welsh fairies travel either above, in the middle of or below the wind. Above is a giddy and terrible sensation, whilst below involves being dragged through bush and brake. This was plainly the experience of one man whose case was described by the Reverend Edmund Jones in the late eighteenth century. A hunting party visited a pub kept by Richard the tailor, "one who resorted to the company of fairies." One of the group went outside to relieve himself and was snatched up by a passing fairy band. He was with them all night, being carried all the way from Monmouthshire to Newport and back again. When he reappeared the next morning, he "looked

---

81 Campbell, *Superstitions,* 69–70 & 87; Evans Wentz, 106; *Old Lore Miscellany,* vol.5, 16; Mackenzie, *Book of Arran,* 258 & 268; MacDougall & Calder, *Folk Tales,* 121; J. Campbell, *Strange Things,* 2006, 267 no.37.
82 Campbell, *Popular Tales,* 79.

like he'd been pulled through thorns and briars." He felt very ill and said that for part of his journey he had been insensible. Evidently, he had been travelling below the wind.[83]

A very similar – and vivid – description of aerial abductions in England was given by Reginald Scot in his *Discoverie of Witchcraft* of 1584:

> "many such have been taken away by the said spirits for a fortnight or a month together, being carried with them in chariots through the air, over hills and dales, rocks and precipices, and passing over many countries and nations in the silence of the night, bereaved of their sense and commonly of their members to boot."[84]

The flying 'chariots' is a unique feature (although we do sometimes hear of ordinary terrestrial carriages and coaches being utilised by the faes) but Scot's depiction of the effect of these prolonged aerial abductions certainly fits very well with the Rev. Jones'. A Manx commentator described those taken as being carried 'insensible' through the sky. Doubtless many of us might faint at the experience. As for his reference to the loss of use of limbs, this may very well have simply been rigid terror induced by the flight, but we shall later consider paralysis as a common feature of faery encounters.

Another reason for the host's flight is to meet with enemies and to fight them. There are numerous accounts of the hosts battling in the sky on cold and frosty nights (most especially at Halloween), leaving pools of blood (*fuil nan sluagh*) on the ground in the morning as testimony to their violent slaughter.[85]

---

83 E. Jones, *The Appearance of Evil,* no.68.
84 Scot, 1584, Book III, c.IV.
85 Watson, 'Celtic Mythology,' *Celtic Review,* vol.5, 1908–9, 59–60; Evans Wentz, 91.

Remedies

The accounts so far, especially that of the man taken despite the best efforts of his friends to prevent it, might suggest that the *sluagh* are pretty much invincible and irresistible. This is not the case, fortunately. Very simple measures can defeat them. Two abductions of women on the Isle of Arran were prevented by means of casting a reaping hook up into the mass of little people as they passed overhead, 'like a swarm of bees.' Being iron, this instantly released the captive being carried away. Likewise, the use of Christian blessings is effective: a Shetland man had flown with the host on a rush by means of simply repeating their spell ("Up hors, up hedik, up well ridden bolwind") and he found himself taken with them to a cottage where a woman was in labour. The plan was to kidnap her if she sneezed three times and no one 'sained' her. She sneezed, but the man riding with the trows instinctively said 'bless you' and so saved her.[86]

Another protection is flax: it was used in the Highlands as a remedy against taking by the *sluagh* and was, significantly, called "the blue-eyed one of the fairy women" ((*gorm-shuileach na mna sith*). Carmichael recorded a spell that was written on a slip of paper worn in a small bag round the neck to accompany the use of the plant, which invokes its powers against the host (*o'n a sluagh is sith*). Prayers and invocations against the menaces of the host are in fact very common in the Highlands, seeking protection from the graces and various saints against the faeries' weapons and against abductions. For example, the saints are beseeched to help against the "sky hosts of evil" (*seun mi bho speurach an uilce*) and from Brigit to ensure that:

"No seed of the fairy host shall lift me,	"*Cha tog siodach mi*
Nor seed of airy host shall lift me."	*Cha tog sluagach mi*"[87]

---

[86] Mackenzie, *Book of Arran*, 258 & 268; Nicolson, *Shetland Folklore*, 82.
[87] Carmichael, *Carmina Gadelica*, vol.3, 109, 133, 161, 182 & 223.

These are magical defences; physical means of resistance tend to be much less certain and much riskier. By way of illustration, some men were tending the herds at Cornaigbeg Farm on Tiree when they heard something passing them on the road. It sounded like a flock of sheep going by, but one of the dogs became very agitated and chased after it. Eventually the poor hound returned – it had lost all its hair and was torn and bloody, dying soon afterwards (see chapter four for more on the antagonism between dogs and faeries).[88]

ELF BOLTS & ELF SHOT

Inextricably linked to the flights of the *sluagh* are the arrows they fire at targets on the ground below. The Scottish folklorist William Grant Stewart, in 1823, described the faeries' use of bolts or arrows as "the most heinous of all their crimes." These very sharp and saw-edged projectiles are thrown by the 'wicked fairies' with great precision and they are always and instantly fatal.[89]

The Reverend Robert Kirk, in *The Secret Commonweath*, made some fascinating and less judgmental remarks about the fairies' habit of shooting 'elf-arrows' at people:

> "Those who are unseened or unsanctified (called Fey) are said to be pierced or wounded with those People's Weapons, which makes them do somewhat verie unlike their former Practice, causing a sudden Alteration, yet the Cause thereof unperceavable at present; nor have they Power (either they cannot make use of their natural Powers, or ask't not the heavenly Aid,) to escape the Blow impendent...

---

88 Campbell, *Popular Superstitions,* 144.
89 W.G. Stewart, *Popular Superstitions... of the Highlanders of Scotland,* 1823, 134–135.

They also pierce Cows or other Animals, usewally said to be Elf-shot, whose purest Substance (if they die) these Subterraneans take to live on, viz. the aereal and ætherial Parts, the most spirituous Matter for prolonging of Life ... leaving the terrestrial behind. The Cure of such Hurts is only for a Man to find out the Hole with his Finger; as if the Spirits flowing from a Man's warme Hand were Antidote sufficient against their poyson'd Dairts."[90]

Two features of Kirk's account are especially striking: one is how the arrows change the people that they strike; the second is his later observation that cattle hit by the fairy arrows can be healed by the laying on of hands.

The firing of elf-bolts was a practice especially associated with the so-called *saighead sith* (the archer fairies) who are numbered amongst the *sluagh sith* or fairy host. They will fly over the length and breadth of the land at night, picking off their chosen targets as they go.

Targets

Elf shots may be released intentionally to kill or abduct people, but also as a way to send warnings to individuals who have violated the faeries' code of conduct. A husband and wife at Herbusta on Skye were harvesting their corn by moonlight one time. The local *sith* folk took exception to this, most probably because they wanted to be left to their own devices, dancing and thieving, on such a night. The man suddenly dropped his sickle, thinking he had cut himself. This injury made him suspect that the faes might have been unhappy so the couple went home for the night. The next day, he found an elf-arrow lying on the stubble at the exact spot where he'd been cut, confirming his suspicions.[91]

---

90 Kirk, chapter 8.
91 Seton Gordon, *The Charm of Skye,* 232.

One particular target of faery animosity, and therefore of elf-shot, is hunters. Because they pursue and kill deer, which provide milk for faery communities in the Scottish Highlands, they are hated and attacked. Another sign of their dislike is that, if a deer *has* been killed, the hunter carrying it home will find the carcase getting heavier and heavier. This is the *sith* pressing down on the body and the only way of dispersing them is to stick a knife into the flesh.[92]

Perhaps the primary function of elf-shot is to kill (or, rather, to steal) cattle. The faeries are fond of beef and mutton and they will acquire their meat by shooting at human herds and flocks. It's said on Shetland that when this happens, the stricken animal is replaced with a 'stock' that isn't fit for human consumption, so the carcases of any beasts suspected of dying through elf-shot will simply be condemned. If an animal becomes dull and costive, it is a sure sign that it has been targeted. Another indicator is that, after the beast has died, the carcase will seem "soft as wool" – very probably because it is not an actual body but some sort of substitute left by the faeries.[93]

Effect

As the last paragraph, and the quotation from Kirk, indicate, the faery arrows are used by the *sith* not as a way of actually killing people or cattle but as a means of abducting them. Numerous examples of this may be found. The practice is described in the Shetland ballad, *King Orfeo,* which is a version of the Middle English poem *Sir Orfeo.* In the ballad –

---

92 Campbell, *Superstitions,* 27–28.

93 'Manners, Traditions & Superstitions of the Shetlanders,' *Fraser's Magazine,* vol.34, 486; *Old Statistical Account of Scotland,* vol.21, 1799, 148 (Monquhitter) & vol.19, 1797, 542, Longforgan, Perth; R. Dinnie, *An Account of the Parish of Birse,* 1865, 35.

"The king, he has a-huntin' gane
An' left his lady all alane
The Elfin King wi' his dairt
Pierced his lady tae the hert..."

King Orfeo's wife doesn't die, though, she is abducted to Elphame. In one reported example, a woman at Glen Cannel on Mull was shot and replaced by a log of alder-wood. To earthly eyes, then, such victims appear to have died, but in reality, their living bodies have been taken. Women were an especial target, but in a case from Gortan in Argyll a cooper was the subject as the fairies needed him to make some barrels.

The actual physiological effect of the arrows seems to be subject to some debate and interpretation. In an early statement, witch-suspect Isobel Gowdie, interrogated in 1662, gave a detailed account of her view of the working of the arrows:

"...we may shoot them dead at owr pleasour. Any that ar shot be us, their sowell will goe to hevin, bot ther bodies remains with us, and will flie as horses to us, as small as strawes."

Scottish witch suspect Jonet Morrison gave a broadly similar description, explaining that "quhen they are schott ther is no recoverie for it and if the schott be in the heart they died presently but if be not at the heart they will die in a while with it yet will at least die with it..." [94]

Folklore authority J.G. Campbell recorded a slightly different opinion, writing that the strike would take the power from the person's limbs, so that they could not defend themselves or escape. Sometimes, they would not die but rather fall ill, in which cases they would have been replaced with an elderly

---

94 Pitcairn, *Ancient Criminal Trials*, vol.3, part 2, 607; McPhail, *Highland Papers*, vol.3, 20–28.

elf who inhabited their body and received care in the victim's stead.[95]

Cattle were taken in very much the same manner as humans. When the elf-bolt strikes a cow, it will be in distress, rolling its eyes and bawling as if suffering from a malignant cramp. A cow struck by an elf-shot may also be identified by the fact that it will be languid, will refuse food and its breathing is laboured. If the shot was not instantly fatal it will leave an indentation on the skin that slowly kills the beast. Either way, when it dies, it is not in fact dead but is rather an effigy that has been left behind and the cow itself has been taken to the fairy knoll. Thus, on Shetland, it used to be said that if a cow or sheep died, it was likely to be because it had been shot with an elf-bolt and replaced with something 'trowie' (in other words, some sort of stock or substitute). Likewise, a living semblance of a cow might be left behind, but it would eat and drink prodigiously without either fattening or producing milk.[96]

Making & Firing the Shot

Elf-bolts have every resemblance to Neolithic flint arrow heads- hence their Gaelic name of *spor sith,* fairy flints. According to witch-suspect Isobel Gowdie, they are made by the devil, who roughs out the shape before passing them to elf-boys who finish them off using a sharp instrument similar to a needle to knap the sharp edges and point.[97]

Humans have always collected elf-shot. Today they may be unwittingly picked up as fascinating antiquarian items, but in the past they had real value. They deflect attacks by elf-shot

---

95 Campbell, *Superstitions,* 27 & 154.
96 Black, *Scottish Charms & Amulets,* 462; Stewart, *Shetland Fireside Tales,* 228; *New Statistical Account of Scotland,* vol.15, 1845, 142 (Sandsthing & Aithsting); Campbell, *Witchcraft,* 91; J. Maxwell Wood, *Witchcraft & Superstitious,* 144.
97 Pitcairn, *Ancient Criminal Trials,* vol.3, part 2, 607 & 615.

shot but are said to have various other curative properties: if boiled in water, they can cure eye disease and ease the pains of childbirth and they are very useful helping to treat afflicted cattle, as we shall see later. Rubbed on wounds, the elf-sot help heal them.[98]

Unfortunately, loosed shots can never be successfully hunted for; rather (just like protective herbs- see chapter five) they will be discovered in unexpected places by accident – for example in the folds of clothing or in shoes or boots. If you do happen to find an arrow, it should not thereafter be exposed to the sun or else the faeries will retake it. Some people think it best to destroy the bolts immediately; some prefer to throw them into lakes or pools or to bury them; some again like to mount the flints and wear them as amulets round their necks. All these practices notwithstanding, Scottish folklorist Alexander Carmichael recorded the opinion that no amount of charms can ever protect arrows from being recovered by the faeries, especially if you have found an arrow shot by the elf queen herself.[99]

There was some difference of opinion as to how the bolts were fired. Some saw them as being just like human arrows. Poet Cromek rather fancifully described how the bows were made from the ribs of men who had been buried at spots where three lairds' lands met, the quivers being made from the sloughed skin of adders and the shafts being fashioned from the stems of bog-reeds. According to Isobel Gowdie, the arrow points were not fired from bows at all, but were rather flipped forcefully from the thumbnail.[100]

In what seems to be a modernisation of this procedure, there is a Shetland report of a woman who was once churning outside her house when she heard something drop into the milk.

---

98 W. Skeat, 'Snake Stones,' *Folklore*, vol.23, 1912, 64; Campbell, *Superstitions*, 27.

99 Black, *Scottish Charms & Amulets*, 462; *Carmina Gadelica*, vol.2, 321.

100 Pitcairn, *Ancient Criminal Trials*, vol.3, part 2, 607.

Inspection revealed this to be an item looking like melted glass, which was believed to be a 'trow gun.' This could be used by the trows to make cattle sick and – it therefore followed – to cure them.[101]

The oddest aspect of the *sluagh*'s hunting expeditions is the fact that the fairies themselves cannot fire their own arrows at their intended victims. They must apparently take a mortal with them to perform this act for them, called a *duine saoghailtre*. Touring Scotland in 1699, antiquary Edward Lhwyd reported to a friend in Surrey that:

> "As to this elf-stricking, their opinion is that the fairies (having not much power to hurt animal bodies) do some-times carry away men in the air, and furnishing them with bows and arrows, employ them to shoot men, cattle etc."[102]

Numerous other sources confirm this curious disability. For example, in one story from the Highlands, a man saw members of the host making a bow and knew that this was for him to use and that they were about to carry him off. He begged his friends to hold him tightly so that he could not be taken, but it happened anyway. The inevitable disadvantage with this reliance is that the human hunter was often reluctant to shoot the targets, often because they knew the person selected. For instance, in the case of the woman from Glen Cannel on Mull, the man taken by the *sluagh* first shot at a lamb, which rose through the window out of the woman's house. The faes were not pleased and he was forced by them to shoot again. In other reported cases, the human captive would deliberately miss or shoot a sheep and a hen instead. As Isobel Gowdie said: "Som tymes we misse; bot if they twitch [touch], be it beast or man or woman, it will kill, tho they had an jack [mail-coat] upon them." She went on, with clear regret: "Bot that quhich troubles

---

101 *www.tobarandualchais.co.uk*, October 6th 1974.
102 Lhwyd, letter from Bathgate to Martin Lister, Leatherhead, Dec.15th 1699.

my conscience most, is the killing of several persones, with the arrowes quhich I gott from the divell."[103]

Protections

Given the constant threat of being shot and taken, what can humans do to protect themselves and their beasts? There were several lines of defence, luckily enough.

Firstly, there are charms that can be recited to protect person and property. On the island of South Uist, for example, a 'herding blessing' used to be sung whilst tending the cattle. It asked St Bridget to protect the stock against a variety of dangers, including "the arrows of the slim fairy women" (*o saighde nam ban seanga sith)*." At his trial for witchcraft in 1607 Bartie Paterson confessed to invoking the holy trinity to guard cattle against "arrowschot" amongst other types of 'shot' directed at them. In the Outer Hebrides, a person would be protected outside if they carried with them a sieve in one hand and a piece of coal in the other, highly inconvenient though this might be. If you were able to come by an elf bolt that had previously been fired, simply carrying that with you was thought to be a complete defence against being struck yourself.[104]

The *Carmina Gadelica* contains numerous invocations against fairy shot, indicating very clearly how real and constant a threat this was considered to be. For example, one charm asks that the breastplate of Columba protect the individual against fairy shafts (*saigheda sith*); another prayer, addressed to the saints John, Peter and James, specifically implores for protection against the "slim and slender fairy darts" (*air na saighde siubhlach sibheideach*).[105]

---

103 Campbell, *Popular Tales*, vol.IV, 310.
104 Campbell, *Strange Things*, 269; A. Campbell, 'Records of Argyll,' *Folklore Record* vol.2 1879, 393; George Low, *A Tour through Orkney & Shetland*, 1889, 17.
105 *Carmina Gadelica*, vol.3, 133, 197 & 223; vol.2 59 and vol.1, 175.

There are various practical steps that can be taken to diminish the risk that you will ever become the target of an attack by the *sluagh*. As mentioned, it's believed that the *sluagh* (and fairies generally) will make their approach from the west. That being the case, leaving westerly windows open after sunset is always a bad idea, because it tempts the *sluagh* to shoot arrows in, especially if a cow is being milked beside that window. Another protection, which is useful where a window is needed for ventilation, is to place an iron bar across it. The iron will stop both fairies and fairy arrows from entering. Many farmers kept broken knives and scythes in their cow byre as a simple protection for their beasts.[106]

Cattle ploughing in the fields were deemed a particular target, but there are simple precautions that can be taken, even when working outside. Both in County Durham, in the North of England, and in Scotland, the practice was to put a bend in the furrows when the fields were being ploughed. The reason for this was said to be that the fairies aimed along the ridges when trying to strike the oxen. The curve simply – but effectively – ruined their aim.[107]

Cures

If, despite charms and physical measures, a cow or a person is still struck, there are various cures that can be administered. In many communities in the past there used to be a 'fairy doctor' who could to detect when sickness arose from being shot with a dart and could then prescribe a remedy. On Shetland, for example, the suspected 'trow-shot' cow would be felt all over. If a dimple, marking the site where the bolt hit, was located, a page of the Bible would be rolled up tightly and put into the

106 J.G. Campbell, *Superstitions*, 69; Campbell, *Strange Things* 269; *www. tobarandualchais.co.uk,* 1960.
107 *Denham Tracts*, vol.2, 146.

depression for a little while. Then it was removed, and with it the cattle's affliction was taken away. Washing the injured cow, rubbing it with stones, or giving it water to drink in which an old elf-arrow had been steeped, are other tried and tested remedies. Putting tar between the cows' horns was also, apparently, helpful; the tar could also be used in cure to glue Bible pages to a beast. Also beneficial were folding a needle in a page and tying it to a cow's hair or using red thread to tie rowan sprigs to its horns; rubbing the injured area with a blue bonnet is also effective.[108]

A woman called Kate of the Tree from Tobermory could cure cows using a fairy dog's tooth and water in which a silver coin had been dipped, their application being combined with a special prayer. Dissolving two tablespoonfuls of salt in a pint of cold water, which is then used to bathe the cow, with a little poured into its ears and down its throat, is helpful. In the absence of silver, an elf-arrow dipped in the water will also be beneficial.[109]

A church minister walking on Foula in the late 1860s witnessed a group of locals dancing and throwing burning brands at a young heifer, whilst reciting a Norse incantation. Questioned as to what they were doing, they told him that the cow had been taken 'into the hill' so they were now trying to drive the trows out of it. Another good cure for trow affliction was a ceremony that involved a burning pan of embers and a wool comb that was run down the cow's back whilst reciting a rhyme. When finished, the beast was struck on its rump and the blow would drive out the trow inside, which would be burned up.[110]

---

108 Haldane-Burgess, 'Some Shetland Folklore,' *Scottish Review*, vol.25, 1895, 99; George Low, *A Tour through Orkney & Shetland,* 1889, 7; F. Barry, 'Charm Stones,' *Folklore,* vol.16, 1905, 336; Home, *County of Caithness,* 1907, 107; 'Manners, Traditions & Superstitions of the Shetlanders,' *Fraser's Magazine,* vol.34, 486.
109 *www.tobarandualchais.co.uk,* 1957; Black, *Scottish Charms & Amulets,* 462.
110 Reid, *Art Rambler in Shetland,* 1869; *www.tobarandualchais.co.uk,* Sept. 28th 1970.

FAIRY FOOD

Fairy foodstuffs are mysterious and dangerous. They look exactly like our own: travellers have often heard (and smelled) bread baking on a griddle or oat cakes toasting before a fire and have felt tempted to eat. However, both eating or drinking food and drink offered to you within fairyland is widely accepted to be a way of ensuring that you cannot escape back to your home; you take fairy nature within yourself and therefore you must abstain from meals whilst visiting. Oddly, though, the converse of this strict rule is that, if you encounter fairy food and drink in the human world, *refusing* to eat it is the perilous thing.

Avoiding food when you're actually in the faeries' home is difficult. Sometimes, a wise friend might warn a person of the risks of eating before they go into Faery – as was the case with a Ross-shire midwife called to a delivery in the knoll at Big Strath; sometimes the help comes from someone in Faerie. In the Hertfordshire fairy-tale of the Green Lady, a girl working as a servant for the green (fairy) woman is warned by fish in a well where she draws water that she should not to eat the household's food. In the same fashion, a man attending a fairy feast on the Isle of Man was warned by one of the other diners (a man he thought he recognised and who was perhaps 'dead' in the human world) not to eat, or else he would never escape either. A Shetland man who joined a dance in a fairy hill received a similar warning and pocketed the food he was given. When he looked at it the following day, he found it was nothing but dried sheep droppings.[111]

There are numerous examples of the potentially fatal consequences of not accepting fairy hospitality when it is offered to us in this world. The ill-effects may, indeed, be more to do

---

111 Robertson, 'Folklore from the West of Ross-shire,' *Transactions of the Gaelic Society of Inverness*, vol.26, 1905, 271; A. Gomme, 'The Green Lady,' *Folklore*, vol.7, 1896, 411; Waldron, *Description of the Isle of Man*, 27; *Old Lore Miscellany, Orkney and Shetland*, vol.3, 1909, 209.

with the offence taken by not eating what you're offered rather than any quality inherent in the goods themselves. The mildest response may be that the faes exact an indirect revenge. On the Isle of Arran two men were ploughing up some fresh land and one joked that the fairies should feed them in recognition of their hard labour. They duly found a table laid at the head of the field, but neither dared eat what had been provided, because of which the field never produced any crops.[112]

A person may suffer physically, though. The least may be physical chastisement: in one story from Devon a ploughman mended a fairy's broken baking peel; cider was left in thanks, which the man happily drank. His plough boy refused it – and was pinched mercilessly.[113] In comparison, in one Scottish account a ploughman felt thirsty and, hearing a butter churn, wished for a drink from it. A woman in green appeared and offered him some fresh buttermilk. He refused this because her clothing made him suspect her supernatural nature. She told him that, after a year had passed, he'd not be needing a drink and, sure enough, within twelve months he was dead. A similar fate befell a man from the Isle of Man who refused to eat some oatmeal porridge offered by the fairies. There is also a variant of the Scottish story involving two men working near a fairy knoll: one refuses the butter milk and dies within the year; the other drinks it gladly and is further rewarded with a wish – which was never to drown. In a third such incident a man from the Isle of Harris passed a fairy knoll at Bearnairidh and heard churning. He was thirsty and wished for a drink, but when a woman in green appeared and offered him fresh milk, he refused it. She cursed him and, very shortly afterwards, he took a boat but drowned when it sank. Prompt retribution seems the more typical outcome: the person refusing the fairy food very often keels over forthwith.[114]

---

112 MacKenzie, *Book of Arran*, 1914, 271.
113 Northcote, 'Devonshire Folklore,' *Folklore*, vol.11, 1900, 213.
114 Campbell, *Popular Tales*, 79; Campbell, *Superstitions*, 137; *Yn Lioar*

Intriguingly, it seems that the refusal to accept the offer of food is what offends, rather than the fact of its ingestion. There is a record of an elderly Scottish woman called Nanzy who had long had friendly dealings with her local fairies. She often met them when she was out and about and they gave her presents, such as rolls of fairy butter. Now, she was too respectable a Christian woman to actually eat this herself, good as it looked, so she instead she sold some of it at market (and never apparently had any customer complaints), whilst she used the rest for other household purposes. These aren't specified in the account, but must have included greasing pans and such like. The case of Nanzy highlights two contradictions for us: firstly, that ingestion whilst in faeryland is the dangerous action, whereas politely refusing a meal (or perhaps only pretending to consume it) doesn't imperil the person in the same way (possibly because they are still to some degree immune to the faeries' powers because they have not eaten). Secondly, it appears to be the outright rejection of the faery offer that riles them: accepting the food but putting it to some other use is for some reason acceptable.[115]

What's the food like, though? Accounts vary. A man from Dornoch in Sutherland was taken by the fairies and flew with them. After this ordeal, they gave him beef, bread and fish to eat, but he complained afterwards that it was like "so much cork."

This report is confirmed, amply, by others: a Perthshire woman who was abducted by the fairies said that the food she was offered looked very tempting, but that when she saw through the glamour, it was "only the refuse of the earth." Another Scottish abductee said grace over a meal and then

---

Manninagh, vol.III, 'Fairies;' E. Watson, 'Celtic Mythology,' Celtic Review, vol.V, 1908–9, 59; Corrie, 'Folklore of Glencairn,' Transactions of Dumfries & Galloway Antiquarian Society, vol.7, 1890, 37.

115 Anon, Notes & Anecdotes Illustrative of the Incidents, Characters & Scenery Described in the Novels of Sir Walter Scott, 1833, 200.

realised that it was nothing but horse dung.[116] In the majority of accounts, however, we're told nothing about the meal itself, and have to assume from this silence that it was exactly like any human repast. At the other end of the scale, one Scottish writer states that fairy bread tastes like the finest wheaten loaf mixed with honey and wine.[117]

A final account fits better with this last report than those that allege that fairy food is nothing but inedible rubbish. Two Shetland fishermen were caught by a storm and had to land their boat on the uninhabited island of Linga. After a few days, conditions improved and one of them men took the boat, deserting his companion Thom. However, that night Thom found a trow banquet taking place in the hut where he was sheltering. The trows tried to chase him off but he resisted and fired his gun, causing the trows to vanish, but leaving behind all their food. He was able to survive extremely well on this for many days until his girlfriend sailed to find him. She had been suspicious when the companion, Willie, returned alone and had tried to marry her, so she carried out a search.[118]

A last thought may turn much of what has just been said on its head, nevertheless. Dafydd William Dafydd was a skilled player on the flute. One day he was out watching his cattle and practicing on his instrument, when he was surrounded by small men. They danced, sang and gave him cakes to eat; Dafydd enjoyed himself very much and thought he spent three hours in their company. To his friends and family, he was absent about three weeks. The cakes here may have been consumed at Bryngrainen Farm, Palleg, Ystradgynlais (on the River Tawe in South Wales) but they appear nevertheless to have been imbued with all the glamour of food eaten in Faery itself.[119]

---

116 Dempster, 'Folklore of Sutherlandshire,' *Folklore Journal*, vol.6, 1888, 220; Grahame *Sketches Descriptive* 111; Campbell, *Superstitions*.
117 Aitken 5; Alan Cunningham, *Remains*, 242.
118 Douglas, *Scottish Fairy & Folk Tales*, 144.
119 S. Hartland, 'Dafydd William Dafydd,' *Folklore Journal*, vol.6, 1888, 191.

FAERIES & CHILDREN

There are several ways in which faeries interact with human children, but it is usually by trying to steal them when they're babies or toddlers, although more rarely they can act contrary to expectation and look after infants where the human parents aren't doing so. Nonetheless, it was once widely understood that the fairies were always on the lookout for chances to abduct infants, so I will focus here on this malign aspect of their culture.[120]

Stealing Babies

The faery predilection for stealing very young infants is well known. The best time to take the child is immediately after its birth, before it has been "touched by mortal hands" or baptised. Special watchfulness is therefore required from families and it used to be the practice for women from a neighbourhood to assemble to watch over the new mother and child. Additionally, nails might be driven into the bed boards and an iron tool might be placed beneath the bed.[121]

The theft of a baby is almost always accompanied by the deposit of a substitute, a faery changeling that may itself be a child or might be an aged person in need of constant care, which the human parents will then supply for free. It hardly needs to be said that there is an almost incalculable cruelty in taking new born infants, although most of this falls upon the parents whilst the child itself is, fortunately, still too young to properly comprehend its situation. It may be some comfort to know that the stolen child is usually very well looked after by its new faery guardians (although very occasionally infants are taken to give to human favourites).[122]

---

120 See, for example, *Evans Wentz* 150 or 'Wee Tommie' in Menzies Fergusson, *Ochil Fairy Tales*, 1912.

121 R. Dinnie, *An Account of the Parish of Birse*, 1865, 35; Campbell, *Superstitions*, 36–37.

122 Dalyell, *Darker Superstitions*, 538; Campbell, *Superstitions*, 23.

However, I have discussed changelings in detail elsewhere, over and above which it is fair to observe that the darkest aspect of this process is probably not the fairies' actions but the human parents' responses. It used to be believed that the only way of persuading (or forcing) the faeries to return the abducted baby was to show great cruelty to the changeling child and, in consequence, a variety of tortures were devised with this aim in mind. This might explain the actions of one James Houston, who was tried on January 22nd 1624 for murdering his grandson; his defence was that he had killed only a substitute and not the real child, for "the fairie had tane him away."[123]

Desirable as babies may be to the faery community, this was not the full story. The trows in particular were noted for their malignant natures. At Dale on Shetland a trow once knocked on the door of a cottage. The housewife looked out to see a strange cow standing in her farm yard and she promptly went to check in her byre that none of her own beasts had got free. In her absence, an arm and hand appeared by the cradle and gave the baby in it a slap on the cheek. This quite gratuitous blow left a mark that stayed into adulthood. In another report, from Soa, near Tiree, a child left alone by its mother when she went out to work had its legs twisted so severely that it was lamed for life.[124]

Kidnapping Juveniles

It's easy enough for the faeries to lift infants out of cradles, but how do they go about making off with older children who can think and act for themselves? There seem to be three broad strategies. The faeries may bodily kidnap them, they may trick them or they may lure them away. There are ample examples

---

123 Dalyell, *Darker Superstitions of Scotland,* 1834, 539, citing *Records of Orkney,* fo.57, verso. For further detail, see my *Middle Earth Cuckoos,* 2021, *Faery,* 2020, c.12 or *British Fairies,* 2017.
124 *Glasgow Herland,* April 9th 1886, 10' 'Shetland Folklore;' Campbell, *Superstitions,* 40 & 85.

to illustrate all of these ploys, so that's it's hardly surprising to discover that it is a longstanding belief that the faeries are always on the lookout for chances to abduct young people. An account from 1908 tells of some Scottish children coming home from school who saw fairies dancing in red in the road. The children weren't captured, but they did have their faces scratched. This could have been punishment for spying on the dance or it might be evidence of a failed kidnap.[125]

Obviously, it's easiest to kidnap children if they come willingly and it is perfectly possible to achieve this by friendly means. In one Scottish example, a little girl had been in the habit of regularly playing with the faeries under the Hill of Tulach at Monzie. One day, however, they cut off a lock of her hair and told her that next time she visited she would stay with them for ever. Fortunately, the child told her mother what had happened and she immediately worked various charms and never let her daughter out to play again. A closely comparable case is reported from Nefyn on the Lleyn peninsula.

"There was one family [living at Nefyn] to which a little girl belonged: they used to lose her for hours every day and her mother was very angry with her for being so much away. 'I must know,' said she, 'where you go for your play.' The girl answered that it was to Pin y Wig (Wig Point') which meant a place to the west of the Nefyn headland: it was there, she said, she played with many children. 'Whose children?' asked the mother. 'I don't know,' she replied; 'they are very nice children, much nicer than I am.' 'I must know whose children they are,' was the reply; and one day the mother went with her little girl to see these children: it was a distance of about a quarter of a mile to Pin y Wig, and after climbing the slope and walking a little along the top they came in sight of the Pin... Now after coming near the

---

125 *www.tobarandualchais.co.uk*, January 10th 1973.

Pin the little girl raised her hands with joy at the sight of the children. 'O mother,' said she, 'their father is with them to-day: he is not with them always, it is only sometimes that he is.' The mother asked the child where she saw them. 'There they are, mother, running down to the Pin, with their father sitting down.' 'I see nobody, my child,' was the reply, and great fear came upon the mother: she took hold of the child's hand in terror, and it came to her mind at once that they were the *tylwyth teg*. Never afterwards was the little girl allowed to go to Pin y Wig because the mother had heard that the *tylwyth teg* exchanged people's children."[126]

What sort of charms might be used by parents to protect their children is shown by the next case. A boy from Borgue in Kirkcudbrightshire had been used regularly to make extended visits to the Good Folk's underground home; he was protected by suspending a crucifix blessed by a Catholic priest around his neck. Indeed, so common could this habit of playing together be that, in one case from Orkney, a little girl so pestered the local trows with repeated visits that, in their irritation, they breathed on her and paralysed her for life.[127]

Simply opening the door to a human child might be enough to tempt it in, then. More often, some additional inducement is necessary. It might be nothing more than playing upon the child's curiosity, as in the Welsh medieval case of Elidyr. He had run away from home after an argument about his lessons and had hidden for two days on a river bank. Two little men then appeared to him and invited him to go with them to "a country full of delights and sports." That was all he required to persuade him to go with them. Somewhat comparable is the tale

---

126 Rhys, *Celtic Folklore*, 275–276.
127 Murray *Tales from Highland Perthshire* no.33; Campbell, *Popular Romances*, vol.1, 425; *County Folklore*, vol.3, 22.

of a boy from St. Allen in Cornwall who was led into Faery by a lovely lady. He first strayed into a wood following the sound of music and, after much wandering, fell asleep. When he awoke, a beautiful woman was with him and she then guided him through fantastic palaces. Eventually he was found by searchers, once again asleep. [128]

Some children require more material temptation to leave familiar and safe places. On the Isle of Man, a girl was walking over a bridge one day when three little men appeared to her and offered her a farthing to go with them. She sensibly refused, knowing that consent would place her in their power for ever. In Northumberland, near Alnwick, there used to be a well-known faery ring. It was reputed that, if children danced round it nine times, they would place themselves in the faeries' control. To encourage children into the ring, the faeries used to leave food and other gifts there and parents, in response, would tie bags containing peony roots and seeds around their offspring's necks as a protection against faery harm. Elsewhere in the north of England, it has been reported that the faeries would leave out lumps of their butter as bait for children. [129]

These inducements to stray start to merge into out-and-out tricks. For example, a boy lost on Dartmoor was found by his mother seated under an oak tree known to be a pixie haunt. He told her that "two bundles of rags" had led him away; they were very evidently pixies in disguise who'd aimed to attract his attention and lull his suspicions. Tellingly, as soon as the lights of his mother's lantern appeared, as she came searching for him, these rags vanished. You may recall from earlier the story from lowland Scotland concerning a girl, sat spinning wool on a distaff by a well, who saw what looked like a pot of

---

128 Evans Wentz has a modern version of the Elidyr story, told to him near Strata Florida – see 148; Hunt, *Popular Romances*, 86, 'The Lost Child.'
129 *Choice Notes & Queries – Folklore*, 1859, 26; Doel, *Folklore of Northumbria*, 18; *Denham Tracts*, vol.2, 138.

gold beneath the surface of the water. She told her father, who suspected it was glamour intended to trap and drown her. The child would evidently have been abducted by the fairies, leaving her seeming corpse in the well for the family to find.[130]

Some children are simply snatched without any ceremony. In one case, from the Isle of Man, a boy sent to a neighbour's house to borrow some candles at night was chased on his way home by a small woman and boy. He ran, but only just kept ahead of them, and when he was back at his home, he had lost the power of speech and his hands and feet were twisted awry. He remained in this state for a week. This could almost be a changeling story, but as we'll see later the loss of speech and bodily function are also strongly suggestive of malign faery contact. In another tale from Man, a ten-year-old girl had a very lucky escape from a similar kidnap attempt. Sent on an errand one day, she was detained by a crowd of little men. Some grabbed hold of her and declared their intention to take her with them; however, others in the party objected to this idea. A fight broke out amongst the faeries and, because they said the child had incited this discord, some of the little men spanked her, but let her get away. The truth of her account was seen in the little red hand prints marking her buttocks.[131]

In extreme cases, children are taken under the guise of some fatal accident. The Maxwell family of Orr in Galloway lost twenty-one children all at once when they were skating on the frozen Loch Edingham. The ice suddenly parted and swallowed the group, before resealing again. The children have been seen since, dressed in green and dancing on the waves. More typically, a single youth is abducted, perhaps by drowning or illness, and a 'stock' is left behind.[132]

---

130 Hunt, *Popular Romances,* 96; Aitken, *A Forgotten Heritage,* 18.
131 Evans Wentz, *Fairy Faith,* 132; Waldron, *Isle of Man,* 39.
132 J. Maxwell Wood, *Witchcraft & Superstitious Record,* 173 – see too 170 & 185.

So far, physical abductions have been discussed, but it must be appreciated that (as with adults) a child's soul can be taken or its mind affected in some way by fairy contact. On Orkney a youngster once went out in a snowstorm. After a while, it returned, completely dry – despite the blizzard – but an imbecile. People were convinced that this change was the work of the fairies.[133]

We have so far been assuming, naturally, that parents would not wish to see their offspring taken to fairyland. One incident contradicts this. A woman from Badenoch in the Highlands was given shelter overnight in a fairy hill but, the next morning, she had to promise to surrender her child to them in return for being set free. She agreed, but was allowed to visit her daughter in the hill. After a while, with no sign of things changing, the infant complained that she had been abandoned by her mother. The woman scolded the girl for suggesting this and the fairies ejected her from the hill and never allowed her in again. This suggestion that fairy abduction might sometimes be a boon for the child is confirmed by another source. The verse 'The Shepherd's Dream,' included in William Warner's *Albion's England,* reveals that changelings were taken from mothers who beat or otherwise abused their progeny.[134]

We should recognise, too, that going with the faeries need not always be prolonged nor unpleasant. Many stories indicate that children will be well cared for in Faery. A game keeper and his wife lived at Chudleigh, on Dartmoor. This couple had two children, and one morning when the wife had dressed the eldest, she let her run off to play while she attended to the baby. In due course, father and mother realised that the girl had disappeared. They searched for days with help from their neighbours, and even bloodhounds, without finding her. One morning several

133 *Old Lore Miscellany,* vol.1, 1907, 247.
134 Campbell, *Popular Tales,* 76; Warner, *Albion's England,* 1612, Book 14, c.91.

days later some young men went to pick nuts from a clump of trees near the keeper's house, and there they came suddenly on the child, undressed, but well and happy, not at all starved, and playing contentedly. The pixies were assumed to have stolen the little girl, but to have cared for her and returned her. [135]

This last paragraph redresses the balance slightly in favour of the fairies. They are not completely heartless – nor immune to the sufferings or entreaties of the bereaved families. One Scottish woman whose grandchild had been taken was passing a fairy knoll one day when she saw the boy inside. She went and asked for the child to be restored to her. The fairies agreed, explaining that he had been left 'unsained' (unblessed) by his parents, which had made him vulnerable. A feast was arranged by the fairies to celebrate his return – and the woman discovered that they had taken her cow to provide the meat. Again, they excused themselves, saying that it too had been left unsained, so that it was the only one they could take (we'll note, too, the apparent absence of any notion that the faeries should use one of their own livestock). They compensated the grandmother with the price of the cow in gold. The moral seems to be that nothing comes for free; there is a price for everything in Faery – even children.

I shall return to this subject in detail later, but many of the basic protections against fairies – *mothan*, iron, blessings and the like – were used to safeguard children. Rhymes were also employed, as in this Shetland example:

> "Hushaba minner's dattie, we shall put the trows awa',
> Broonie shanna get the bairn
> And if he comes the cocks'll craa." [136]

---

135 Northcote, 'Devonshire Folklore', *Folklore*, vol.11, 1900, 213.
136 *www.tobarandualchais.co.uk*, August 8th 1961.

Faery Playmates?

There's also evidence of faeries befriending lonely young people working as servants and farm maids and entertaining them with music, dance and company. I'll cite three cases, all from the west of Britain. John Rhys tells the story of Eilian of Garth Dorwen, near Carmarthen. She was hired by an elderly couple to help on their farm. However well treated she was, Eilian was probably lonely without company of her own age and she got into the habit of spinning outside in a meadow by moonlight, where the *tylwyth teg* would visit her and sing and dance as she worked. Eventually, the girl disappeared with the Fair Family and it later turned out that she had been taken to be a fairy wife.[137] Very close to this story is that of Shui Rhys of Cardiganshire. She looked after her parents' cows and often stayed out in the fields very late. She was told off by her mother for this and blamed the spirits, saying that little people in green would come to her, dance and play music around her and speak to her in a language she couldn't understand. These contacts were allowed to continue, for fear of offending the fairies, but it was a risky strategy and, eventually, Shui disappeared just like Eilian.[138]

The story of Anne Jeffries from Cornwall is comparable to these. She had deliberately gone out, trying to make contact with the fairies by repeating little verses to summon them, and eventually they came to her in her garden. Six little men in green appeared to her one day, showered her with kisses – and then carried her off to Faery. She stayed there only a short while, until a violent dispute arose over her affections, after which she was ejected, but the fairies continued to favour her with healing knowledge and a supply of food. It's interesting to remark that in Anne's case, just as in that of the Manx girl who got spanked, faery opinion over the presence of humans in their world could

---

137 Rhys, *Celtic Folklore*, 211–212.
138 Sikes, *British Goblins* 67–69.

be divided and could provoke strong emotions that triggered infighting.

These examples must all be viewed ambivalently, too, as the fairies' great friendliness to these isolated girls seem to have been a pretext for lulling their suspicions prior to abducting them. The fairies of Annandale, for instance, were well known for taking young men and women to act as slaves, beasts of burden and servants. Such ulterior motives may well sound rather more familiar and fit rather better with the impression of faery character that most folk accounts give.[139]

Even if the fairies are acting sociably, and simply want to keep a lonely person company, their friendship will still come with the usual caveats and rules. Enys Tregarthen told the story of 'The boy who played with fairies.' He lived alone with his mother on St Columb Moor in mid-Cornwall and had no playmates. The fairies came to see him daily in a secluded place on the moor and kept him company – on condition that he never told his mother. In due course she demanded to know where he went to every day and, on confessing his secret, lost his fairy friends for ever. This secrecy may just have been faery habit, but it may equally have been part and parcel of a longer-term plan at abduction, somewhat like the girl from the Hill of Tulach near Monzie discussed earlier.

Summary

Fairies may appear amicable and accommodating, therefore, but this is often done with a view to what might be obtained in return. Fairy authority Katharine Briggs, in her 1978 book *Vanishing People,* gave this rather harsh summary of the fairy temperament:

---

139 J. Maxwell Wood, *Witchcraft & Superstitious Record,* 185.

"the kindness of the fairies was often capricious and little mercy mingled with their justice... We are dealing with a pendulous people, trembling on the verge of annihilation, whose mirth is often hollow and whose beauty is precarious and glamorous. From such, no great compassion can be expected."[140]

Fairy friendship may be extended to children, but they should always approach it with great caution. The faes' amity towards humans may not be as open and free as we would expect from other people.

In conclusion, as is often the case, the overall impression we get of the faery relationship with humans is one of contrariety and unpredictability. They may care for our children if they're neglected, but they have absolutely no qualms about kidnapping them in other situations. They take good care of their own families, look after the children they kidnap, and appreciate it when humans tend for faery infants, but they can also behave quite heartlessly towards the young. This is just another example of how complex our dealings are with the Good Folk and how careful we need to be.

---

140 Briggs, *Vanishing People*, 161.

CHAPTER TWO

Fairy Dominance

In many respects, the magical power of faeries means that they effectively control people's lives. The influence they have upon our daily affairs may manifest itself through direct interventions or it may be expressed through the adaptations that people make to accommodate themselves to the faery presence. This may be seen in decisions as to where they go, what they say and how they conduct themselves.

FAERY THIEVERY

This subject was mentioned in the introduction but it is important to confront the matter. The faery glamour and invisibility discussed in the previous chapter are deployed, as often as anything, to deprive humans of their possessions.

Protective as they are of their own goods, rights and privacy, the faes seem to lack any empathy with humankind and are unable to apply similar instincts to us. The have a strict moral code that they impose upon their mortal neighbours but, as Katharine Briggs observed, a key tenet of this is "All that's yours is mine, all that's mine is my own."[1]

During this book I shall allude repeatedly to faery larceny, but a few quotations from Professor John Rhys' *Celtic Folklore* will underline the very poor reputation that our Good Neighbours have and which applies across the length and breadth of the British Isles. One of Rhys' informants was a William Jones of Llangollen, who had written extensively in Welsh on the *tylwyth*

---

1 Briggs, *Dictionary of Fairies*, 154, 'Fairy Morality.'

teg. North Welsh tradition was that they were "of a thieving nature." The *tylwyth* "were wont to frequent fairs and to steal money from the farmer's pockets, where they placed in its stead their own fairy money, which looked like the coin of the realm but when it was paid for anything bought it would vanish in the pockets of the seller... They would lurk around people's houses, looking for an opportunity to steal butter and cheese from the dairies and they skulked around the cow-yards, in order to milk the cows and goats – which they did so thoroughly that there was not a drop of milk to be had." The faeries stole from shops and from stalls at markets and fairs, from cottages, houses and from farms, so that all in all "they were thieves without their like."[2]

Elsewhere, Rhys reported the belief in Cardiganshire that the *tylwyth teg* would steal whatever took their fancy, "for thieving was always natural to them; but no-one ever complained, as it was supposed to bring good luck." Perhaps this is making the best of a bad job, but the notion may possibly be that the faery contact will prove beneficial to the household or individual.[3]

FAE CONTACTS

We turn now to consider the places in which faeries might be encountered, wielding their magical powers. It may, of course, be highly inadvisable to wish to meet with our Good Neighbours, but what is absolutely sure is that we can never plan or intend to meet them. Many authorities on the subject have agreed on this. Janet Bord, in *Fairies – Encounters with Little People*, wrote that:

> "Very often, people who see fairies come across them suddenly and unexpectedly; certainly, they are not thinking about them at the time of the encounter. It may be that a

2 Rhys, *Celtic Folklore*, 82–83.
3 Rhys, *Celtic Folklore*, 251.

certain detachment of mind may be a prerequisite to having what is clearly some kind of psychic experience, and the lone traveller is well placed to be in a receptive condition."[4]

Seventeenth century antiquary John Aubrey agreed with this modern opinion. He wrote in his *Natural History of Wiltshire* that:

"indeede it is saide they seldom appeare to any persons who go to seeke for them."

The fairies choose whether and when to reveal themselves to mortals, appearing and disappearing at will. All of these foregoing observations are confirmed – and explained – by lines in John Lane's pastoral poem of 1621, *Triton's Trumpet*. He explains that:

"... none that breathe living aier doth knowe,
Wheare is that happie land of Faerie...
For it is movable of Mercurie,
Which Faeries of a trice do snatch up hence,
Fro' sight and heering of the common sense;
Yet coms on sodaines to the thoughtlesse eye
And ear (favoured to heer theire minstrelsy),
Ne bootes climbe promontories yt to spie,
For then the Faeries dowt the seeing eye
Onlie right sold it to some fewe doth chaunce,
That (ravish'd) they behold it in a traunce..."[5]

Lastly, the Cornish fairy writer Enys Tregarthen, in her 1911 story entitled *Hunting Fairies*, indicated that a human will never find pixie gold by deliberately searching for it. Having failed to

---

4 Bord, *Fairies – Encounters with Little People*, 35.
5 John Lane, *The Triton's Trumpet*, cited in Halliwell, *Illustrations of the Fairy Mythology*, c.XV.

locate treasure by watching for pixies digging, her character Carveth throws away his pick axe carelessly. He is then advised to dig wherever it happened to fall – and by this means he finds a crock of coins.

What can we learn from these scraps of information? As we know very well, the fairies are a secretive and private people who don't like to be intruded or spied upon. We assuredly can't petition them, praying for them to give us things or to make our wishes come true. Equally, it should be clear that we can't plan to meet or to take advantage of them. They may choose for their own reasons to reveal themselves or to enrich those whom they decide to favour, but they aren't to be begged or imprecated. They are in control, over those whom they help and those to whom they reveal themselves.

The fairies are everywhere; they are among us, at all times and in all places. When we address them as our Good Neighbours, the reference to their proximity is not idle politeness but a simple statement of fact. This reality was well known to previous generations, but the knowledge has been obscured for us now because of urbanisation and the dislocation of rural traditions. For our ancestors, though, the faeries were ever-present in their environment and they reacted to this fact by taking constant precautions to keep away from the 'Good Folk' and to minimise all possibility of antagonising them.

On Shetland, folklorist Eliza Edmonston recorded in her 1809 book *Sketches and Tales of the Shetland Islands* (and with some irritation on her part at their gullibility) how amongst the local people:

> "the knolls under which these 'good people' congregate, the solitary springs whence they fetch water and the especial evenings on which they busy themselves in mundane matters, are all heedfully noted and, at any other risk, avoided."[6]

---

6 *Sketches & Tales* 22

Faery encounters all about luck (whether good or bad). If you hunt them, they'll certainly elude you; if you take what comes, you may be rewarded – or you may be punished. Faery encounters are ambivalent and, generally, it is not advisable to openly pursue them. Our forebears were well aware of the equivocal nature of faeries and preferred to keep them at arm's length. Our modern romanticisation of Faery, the suggestion that they are the natural companions of children, the idea that they might be the playmates of butterflies and bunnies, and the blithely celebratory tone of a poem like Rose Fyleman's *There are fairies at the bottom of our garden* would have been entirely alien to them. Our ancestors had a more honest and brutal sense of faery nature and, had they discovered faeries living in such close proximity to their homes, they would probably have been alarmed and considered moving away as soon as they could, rather than being thankful that they "they'd dare to come merrymaking there" and expressing a fervent hope that "they've really come to stay."

Scottish expert John Gregorson Campbell expressed the traditional view succinctly and severely: "It is unfortunate even to encounter any of the race, but to consort with them is disastrous in the extreme." He continued in equally gloomy and admonitory tones:

"Mortals should have nothing to do with any of the race. No good comes out of the unnatural connection. However enchanting at first, the end is disaster and death. When, therefore, the [fairy] is first met, it is recommended by the prudent to pass by without noticing; or, if obliged or incautious enough to speak, and pressed to make an appointment, to give fair words, saying, 'If I promise that, I will fulfil it' (*ma gheallas mi sin, co-gheallaidh mi e*), still sufficiently near houses to attract the attention of the dogs. They immediately give chase, and the fairy flies away."

Even for midwives and wet-nurses, whose stay in Faery is of limited duration and is remunerated, Campbell warned that "none of them was ever the better ultimately for her adventure."[7]

RIDING HUMANS

Fairies are reputed to ride a variety of creatures. It is very well known from the folklore that fairies and pixies like to take horses from stables and ride them at night, returning the steeds distressed, sweating and exhausted in the morning. On Skye it has been reported that the faeries would gallop farm horses in perilous places at night, the risk being multiplied by the fact that the riders sat facing the tail. Often, too, the horses' manes will be fiendishly knotted to make stirrups and panniers for their faery riders.[8]

A witch-stone or hag-stone (a naturally holed stone) hung just above the animals in their stalls will prevent this. Sprays or crosses of birch put over a stable door will bar the faeries from entering at night. Horses heard to neigh at night are being ridden too hard by the faes: the solution is for the person hearing the cries of distress to shout out "your saddle and pillion be upon you," which will instantly make the faeries fall off.[9]

Often, on Shetland, when cattle were released from their byres to graze in the spring, one would be found that was weak and frothing at the mouth. It was understood that they were in this condition because they too had been ridden by the trows.[10]

Faery Ridden

Be warned, though: if the faeries want to go out riding and there are no suitable steeds to hand, they can use us instead.

---

7   Campbell, *Superstitions*, 23, 40 & 41.
8   See my *British Pixies*, 2021, c.7.
9   Campbell, *Superstitions*, 30.
10 *www.tobarandualchais.co.uk*, Sept. 28th 1970.

Especially on the Isle of Man, people have been known to be taken and ridden all night. They feel no weight on their backs during the experience, but they become tired from loss of sleep and thin and weak from their exertions. Luckily, it is said that taking the precaution of wearing a suitable flower or herb to scare off the faeries (rowan blossom say) should be enough to prevent this.[11]

By way of illustration, we hear of a woman from the Isle of Arran who suddenly fell ill and became very fatigued and sleepy. Her family suspected that this was no ordinary tiredness and watched her at night. They discovered that the fairies were coming when the rest of the household was asleep and were turning her into a horse, which they then used for their carting. A search of the garden the next morning uncovered a hidden harness, which helped break the spell cast upon her.[12]

Hag Ridden

A related closely concept appears to exist in Scotland. Earlier, when examining the elf-bolts shot off by the *sluagh*, we considered the confession of suspected witch Isobel Gowdie that she had gone out with the host to shoot elf-bolts at hapless humans. These random victims were then put to use she said:

> "Any that ar shot be us, their sowell will goe to Hevin, bot ther bodies remain with us, and will flie as horsis to us, as small as strawes."

These straw-like beings were used by the witches to ride upon, just like horses. They sat astride them, pronounced 'horse and hattock' and then travelled in a whirlwind. Real straws and plant stems might also be enchanted for this purpose, whence the idea of broomsticks. This mode of travel is a favourite of

11 See my *Manx Faeries,* 2021.
12 W. MacKenzie, *Book of Arran,* 267.

witches: see for instance the testimony of Bessie Flinkar, tried in 1661, who travelled to covens this way and the accusation made against Bessie Skebister of Orkney in 1633 that she had ridden a man at night with a bridle in his mouth – at a time when he appeared to be very ill with distemper. However, these were also powers possessed by those with the second sight and this is, of course, exactly what the fairies were very commonly known to do.[13]

In former times it was widely believed that wasting illness and perpetual tiredness (symptoms we might now ascribe to a poor diet or to underlying health conditions) were actually the result of being 'hag ridden' – turned into horses by witches, or fairies, and ridden at night. An alternative explanation was that the person was being carried off nightly to dance under the fairy hill. Either way, their energy was being drained and they received no rest when they seemed to be asleep.

To conclude, therefore: we must not be complacent. Almost any available object can be employed by the faeries to travel about. Plant stems are regularly enchanted with their glamour, they keep their own horses, but they will just as readily take steeds kept by humans from their stables and, most alarmingly, they may even cast a spell on us and exploit us.

SERVANTS OF THE FAIRY QUEEN

We know that fairies will take human lovers, especially the Faery Queen, and we know too that these lovers may prove to be possessive and vindictive partners (the *leannan sith* of the Scottish Highlands and the *lhiannan shee* Isle of Man are consistently portrayed this way). One aspect of these relationships that often receives less attention is the need, or desire, for the human partner to make a binding commitment

---

13 John Aubrey, *Miscellanies*, 158; Pitcairn, *Ancient Criminal Trials*, vol.3, 604; for Skebister, see Dalyell, *Darker Superstitions*, 470 & 512 et seq.

to the fairy monarch who becomes their lover or teacher. Nonetheless, it is a consistent (if not common) aspect of many of these stories – and it is recorded from an early date.[14]

Medieval Examples

In the fifteenth century ballad of *Thomas of Erceldoune*, the hero is approached by the fairy queen one sunny May morning when he is out, walking alone in the countryside near Melrose. He is instantly taken by her beauty and declares, impetuously, "Here my trouth I plight thee, Whedur thou wilt to heven or hell..." Initially, this rash display of subservience appears to have achieved its purpose, because an extended sex session follows. However, intercourse with the fairy queen isn't to be undertaken lightly and isn't consequence free: once she's recovered from his over-energetic attentions, the queen declares that he's going with her to fairyland for the next twelve months. There are no ifs or buts about this; she tells him bluntly:

> "For thy trowthe thou hast me tane,
> Ayene that may ye make no stryfe."

Thomas has made an oath and bound himself to her – and now he's stuck with it.

Something similar is found in Thomas Chestre's *Sir Launfal*. The knight is summoned into the presence of fairy lady Tryamour and once again a commitment is extracted from the human in the hope of getting inside her bodice (as well as becoming wealthy): she tells him:

> "Yf thou wylt truly to me take,
> And alle wemen for me forsake,
> Ryche I wylle make thee..."

---

14 On faery lovers, see my *Love and Sex in Faeryland*, 2021.

This is more than just a promise of true love from Sir Launfal. He has to pledge to keep their liaison secret, in return for which, as well as her body, he gets a purse full of gold that will never run out.

Scottish Cases

The examples from romantic literature are supplemented forcefully by the recorded experiences of men and women suspected of witchcraft in early modern Scotland. It's a regular, if not frequent, aspect of these cases that contact with the faeries involved some sort of binding commitment by the human. Firstly, in 1576 in Ayrshire Bessie Dunlop admitted that she had met a fairy man called Thom Reid who had asked her to 'trow' (trust in) him and to give up Christianity, in return for which she would receive livestock and other material assets. She had refused to do this, but she had offered to be true to him in every other way.[15]

Marion Grant of Aberdeen was tried in 1597 for her contacts with a fairy man she called Christsonday. Twelve years previously he had come to her and asked her to call him lord and become his servant – to which Marion consented. Sexual intercourse followed, after which she would be visited by him monthly. She admitted that she worshipped him on her knees and that he taught her healing powers in return. The next year in the same city Andro Man confessed to a relationship with the fairy queen that had lasted over three decades and had produced a number of children. One sign of his commitment (and submission) to her had been to kiss her "airss" on Rood-day in harvest the year before.[16]

Margaret Alexander of Livingston in 1647 confessed to a thirty-year affair with the fairy king, at the start of which he had required her to renounce her baptism as a demonstration

---

15 Pitcairn, *Ancient Criminal Trials*, vol.1, 49–58.
16 *Spalding Club Miscellany*, vol.1, part 3, 117–122 and 170.

of her commitment to him. Lastly, in 1677 at Inverary, Donald McIlverie was tried for the "horrid crime of corresponding with the devil." This wasn't an exchange of letters, of course, but regular visits to a fairy hill where he danced and spoke with the folk living inside. They helped him find stolen goods, in return for which Donald had to agree to keep their involvement secret and, in addition, to tell them his name – which he avoided doing. He knew that this would have bound him irrevocably to them, but in the event his commitments to them were enough to ensure his conviction and execution.[17]

A final example of this kind of contract or pact comes from the other end of the country, from Rye in Sussex on the English south coast. Here, in 1607, a woman called Susan Snapper received repeated visits from a group of fairies, who promised her wealth and good fortune, primarily by guiding her to buried treasure. However, on one occasion, it appeared that there was a price for this. She had been taken to a field of rye near the town where she was told two pots of gold coins were buried. Whilst she was there, she saw two other people, a man in black and a woman in green. Her fairy guide told her that the woman was the fairy queen and that "if she woulde kneele to her shee would give her a living." On that day, however, the two figures vanished and Susan made her way home feeling ill and took to her bed. It did not seem that the offer was repeated to her.[18]

More Recent Examples

Binding promises to the fairies are by no means a thing of the past. They are still to be found in much more recent folklore accounts, although the terms of the commitments seem to have changed somewhat.

---

17 A. Macdonald, 'A Witchcraft Case of 1647,' *Scottish Law Times*, April 10th 1937, 77–78; McPhail, *Highland Papers*, vol.3, 1914, 36–38.

18 G. Slade Butler, 'The Appearance of Spirits in Sussex,' in *Sussex Archaeological Collections*, vol.14, 1862, 25–34.

In a well-known Scottish story from the nineteenth century, a seal hunter living near John O'Groats is visited one night by a stranger on horseback who urgently wants to agree a sale of seal skins. The hunter readily agrees to go with the man to inspect the skins and climbs up on his horse, but it gallops off at unnatural speed and plunges over a cliff into the sea. They sink down to an underwater realm where the hunter is confronted with a selkie man whom he had seriously injured with his knife earlier that same day. Only the man can heal the wound he has inflicted, which he does (having little option in the circumstances). He is released from the selkies' cavern, but only after making a solemn oath never to hunt seals again.[19]

In the Scottish story of Whuppity Stoorie a fairy woman cures a family's sickly pig, but in return she demands their baby – unless they can discover her name. Very close to this is the English tale of Tom Tit Tot, who undertakes to carry out an impossible amount of flax spinning for a young woman, on condition that she will become his – unless again she can guess his name.

In the older stories, the pledge to the fairy monarch took the form of what was essentially a feudal oath of fealty – just as knights would give to their lords and those lords would give to their king. In more modern accounts, it seems that the fairies have moved with the times and the commitment they exact is more contractual in nature: there is an exchange between the parties, however disproportionate the payment demanded by the fairy.

When we read about love affairs with fairy partners, whether of short or long duration, we tend to imagine them in terms familiar to us: in other words, we conceive of an exchange of love and affection and an emotional bond between the parties. Such love matches definitely take place between humans and faes, although, given what we saw of the spells for conjuring

---

19 T. Keightley, *Fairy Mythology*.

faery lovers, we may suspect that many human males, at least, have an eye to the material advantages to be gained from these partnerships. As often, though – and most especially in cases where your lover is a faery monarch – the arrangement ought to be viewed more as a transaction or business deal. To repeat what was said earlier, sex with the faery king or queen may not come for free; a binding commitment may be required and this may be couched in terms rather different to those of the marriage vows.

CHAPTER THREE

Faery Reprisals

So far, we have discussed the faeries' active propagation of loss and damage in the human world. They may also cause similar harm in response to perceived infractions of their rights, liberties and status. Mortals can innocently aggravate the faes by simply going about their daily business and so bring supernatural retribution upon themselves. That said, humans are not, of course, merely passive subjects or victims: they can retaliate to faery interference and may then face further meddling, or, worse.

The vengeful nature of faeries needs to be set against a wider assessment of their character. They must be regarded as naturally combative and aggressive – for example, some Shetland girls once recalled seeing two bands of trows fighting. The children had been playing in a ruined house when two groups of male trows, one white and one black, appeared and attacked each other for an extended period before vanishing. This aggressiveness appears to be combined with a perverse delight in being awkward and intimidating. Orrick in North Voe on the Shetlands was known to be especially haunted by the trows. A man who had been visiting his father there set off for his own home after dark one evening. He found himself surrounded by trows and his way blocked. He retreated to his father's home for help, but the two together were unable to drive the trows away and they had to give up.[1]

Given their predilection for fighting amongst themselves, it will hardly surprise us to learn that unprovoked faery attacks against humans are the norm. These may take place

---

1 Narvaez, *Good People*, 134; *Shetland Folk Book*, vol.3, 1957.

adventitiously or they may be periodic. In Lancashire, the Townley Hall boggart is quite typical of a class of vicious and marauding sprites who regularly demand a human life. The boggart appears in every seventh year, seeking the death of one of the residents of the hall. Several river sprites are notorious too for taking a life every couple of years.[2]

Such is faery nature that even basic dealings with them might be framed in terms of conflict. For example, in the mid-seventeenth century a woman called Jean Weir was teaching at Dalkeith when she was approached by another who proposed "That the declarant should imploy her to spick for her to the Queen of Farie, and strik and battle in her behalf with the said Queen."[3]

FAIRY VENGEANCE

One of the major perils of crossing the fairies is that they can be very likely to seek revenge. They have a vindictive and instinctively retaliatory streak, something which is not alleviated at all by their generally indifferent or uncaring attitude to humankind. We must add to this the problem that they are immortal: the fairies can wait to get their own back, not just through the perpetrator's lifetime, but far down the generations (as Professor John Rhys described). He speculated whether this delayed gratification was the result of their deathlessness or because some spell or magical prohibition prevented prompter action on their part.[4]

Rhys illustrated the vengeful aspect of the faery character with an account from Pantannas, near Beddgelert. A man sought to banish the *tylwyth teg* from his farm by ploughing up all the

2 T. Wilkinson, 'On the popular customs and superstitions of Lancashire, Part 2,' *Transactions of the Historic Society of Lancashire and Chesire,* vol.12, 1859–60, 92.
3 Dalyell, *Darker Superstitions,* 536.
4 *Celtic Folklore* vol.I, c.VII & vol.II 420–25.

areas of grass sward (so that, effectively, they had nowhere left to dance). The farmer immediately began to see apparitions, or to hear voices, threatening that *"Dial a ddaw"*, 'Vengeance is coming.' Soon afterwards, all his supply of corn was destroyed by fire, but the fairies declared this to be only the beginning of their inexorable and inflexible revenge. The farmer restored the grassy areas he had destroyed and pleaded with the *tylwyth teg* for mercy, and they returned to the land, but the threat of further action was not lifted – it was only postponed to his descendants. A century later, the warning voices were heard again (*'Dial a ddaw'*) and, soon enough, the vengeance was exacted. The son of the family disappeared at night, presumed to have been taken by the *tylwyth teg* at a fairy ring, and he was not seen again for several generations. When he finally returned, the world was utterly changed and his name was only a dim memory and – as we've seen so often happens in Welsh stories – as soon as he touched something in the mortal world, he crumbled away to dust. What we gather from this is that the faeries won't forget and that, to make matters worse, they are patient, so that wholly innocent future generations may pay the price of any forbear's foolhardiness.

Lewis Spence summarised the uneasy relationship with the faes in these terms: it is "essential to keep on good terms with the fairies in a social sense. They were usually good neighbours, but relentless enemies."[5] In truth, any dealings at all are perilous: John Campbell warned that "their gifts have evil influences and, however inviting at first, are productive of bad luck in the end."[6]

Rudeness & Meanness

A variety of offences will incur their wrath. The faeries object to anything that they consider as unneighbourly or unfriendly

---

5   Spence, *British Fairy Origins*, 30.
6   Campbell, *Superstitions of the Scottish Highlands*, 23.

behaviour. Thus, refusing loans to the fairies is very likely to spark their enmity. In County Durham it is said that the fairy queen lives at Clint's Crag in Weardale, in a cavern. She often used to be seen by local women, because she would visit their homes to borrow kitchen utensils. People knew not to refuse, as she would take revenge if she could not get what she wanted. Evidently, the rank of faery queen is not so elevated that the monarch is supplied with all her wants nor is she freed from the chore of having to satisfy these needs herself.[7]

Refusing to provide other assistance to the faeries is similarly unadvisable. A Scottish woman from Livingstone, Barbara Parish, was executed in May 1647 for her associations with the Good Neighbours. In one case, she stated that the faeries had come to see her, looking for a wet nurse for one of their babies. Parish had suggested they approach her neighbour, but the woman refused to go with them. Her own child died as a result and the 'green women' inflicted sickness on Parish's neighbour too.[8]

Into this category of offence fall such actions as failing to leave water out for the Good Neighbours when they visit a human home at night. When one family forgot one evening to put out water, soap and towels for the *tylwyth teg*, as was habitual, the peeved fairies overturned their stacks of peat outside. The necessity of observing the custom is made keener by the fact that faeries may take human blood of there is no water available for them.[9]

The faeries also expect many householders to provide them with bread and milk (or cream) and any breach of this convention will incur their wrath. A man and his wife had been in the habit of providing the faeries who frequented their home with a little loaf of the finest white bread and a basin of sweet cream. Sadly,

---

7 Brockie, *Legends & Superstitions of County Durham*, 86.

8 A. Macdonald, 'A Witchcraft Case of 1647,' *Scots Law Times*, April 10th 1937, 77–78.

9 *Y Cymmrodor*, vol.7, 1886, 196; J. G. Campbell, *Superstitions of the Highlands*, 20.

the first wife died and, after the widower remarried, his new wife thought she could make some economies in the household budget. She therefore set out a wholemeal loaf and a herring's head. She was pulled out of bed and down the stairs by the faeries, who chanted "Brown bread and herring cobb! Thy fat sides shall have many a bob!"[10]

Anything that suggests meanness towards the faes – and an unwillingness to share with them – will violate their code of morality. Thus, a couple out walking on the Isle of Man met a small, crippled man begging. Whilst the wife would have helped, the husband refused to give him any money, for which he was cursed. They had a number of children subsequently – all the girls were born without disabilities, but all the boys were disabled just like the beggar. In another Manx story, a man realised that the someone was stealing potatoes from his field after dark. He decided to sit out all night to catch the culprit. He discovered it was the fairies and, by the next morning, he was white and shaking and only able to struggle home and get into his bed, where he soon died. This was the penalty for begrudging a few spuds. A third Manx story concerns a girl baking at Bride. She forgot the custom of sharing the resulting oat cake with the Little People but when she went up to sleep and got into bed, she received a blow to her face. She knew this was a message from the fairies, so she went straight back down, baked a new cake and shared it as tradition required.[11]

Disclosing faery aid can be harshly treated. People are often chosen to be the recipients of gifts of small sums of money and it is widely understood that to reveal or boast about the source of one's good fortune will result in the finds of coins terminating. In a couple of Welsh examples, though, admitting that the tylwyth teg were the benefactors was judged far more harshly. A

---

10 W. Scott, *Letters*, VII.

11 Roeder, *Manx Folklore*, 1882–5; *Proceedings of the Isle of Man Natural History & Archaeology Society, vol.1, Jan. 1889*; *Yn Lioar Manninagh*, vol.2, 194

girl living on a farm at Llangeinwen on Anglesey in about 1815 used to dance with the Fair Family and would receive presents of money in return. Her father demanded to know where she was going at night and where she was getting the coins from, presumably fearing prostitution. She refused to speak, on pain of death. He threatened to beat her unless she confessed, which she did – and died the very same day. A man from Pen y bont near Corwen was another recipient of faery bounty, until his wife insisted that he explain his improved fortunes. He too died soon after doing as she asked.[12]

Trying to exploit any assistance from the fairies is also unadvisable. If the fairies are helping an individual, that person's requests should never be excessive or unreasonable. An example of how such presumption may be punished comes from Hafod Rugog in North Wales. This place was:

> "in a wild hollow among the mountains, where the fair family were in the habit of resorting, and that they used to trouble the old woman of Hafod for the loan of one thing and another. So, she said, one day, 'You shall have the loan if you will grant me two first things: that the first thing I touch at the door break, and that the first thing I put my hand on in the house be lengthened half a yard.' There was a grip stone (carreg afael), as it is called, in the wall near the door, which was in her way, and she had in the house a piece of flannel for a jerkin which was half a yard too short. But, unfortunately, as she came, with her creel full of turf on her back, to the house, she nearly fell down – she put her hand, in order to save herself, to her knee-joint, which then broke; and, owing to the pain, when she had got into the house, she touched her nose with her hand, when her nose grew half a yard longer."[13]

---

12 Y Cymmrodor, vol.9, 1886, 384; Archaeologia Cambrensis, 5th series, vol.3, 1886, no.9, 72.

13 M. de Garis, Folklore of Guernsey, 1975, 157; Rhys, Celtic Folklore, 107.

This incident typifies the faeries' sense of justice, their tendency to take humans' words too literally and their cruel practical joking.

Refusing help offered by the faeries can have disastrous consequences, too. It's understandable why people might decline this aid, for as has already been remarked, such offers are unlikely to be disinterested. Nonetheless, a cautious response must be balanced by consideration of their reaction to it, as one farming family in Clackmannanshire found out. David Wright of Craiginnin farm had long benefitted from the faeries doing his haymaking. At shearing time, he repaid them with a few fleeces and the arrangement continued to the satisfaction of both sides for many years. When David died and son inherited the farm, the young man scorned the help of the "green goons" and had his own men cut the meadows. In response, the faeries nightly scattered his freshly cut hay. He retaliated by ploughing up their rings and knolls but they responded in turn by causing all his livestock to sicken and die. Finally, the younger Wright was travelling home in the dark one night, became lost and was drowned.[14]

It follows that rejecting an offer of faery food is likely to be very poorly received. There are sound reasons for a human declining such an offer: the firm belief is that consuming faery food or drink functions to unite the person with the faes and so will render the individual incapable of returning to his/her mortal life.[15] Nonetheless, the rejection is always treated as a slight by the faes – an impossible dilemma for the subject, as a Scottish incident illustrates. Two men were out scything hay one day. A faery woman appeared and offered them buttermilk to drink. One man accepted the drink and thereafter enjoyed a prosperous, albeit short, life. His companion was too scared to drink and was cursed.[16]

---

14 *County Folklore*, vol.7, 311.
15 Spence, *British Fairy Origins*, 69 & 79.
16 *www.tobarandualchais.co.uk*, 1969 & August 1968; J. Maxwell Wood, *Witchcraft & Superstitious Record*, 183.

Trespasses & Intrusions

Any action, however unintentional, that appears to violate the faeries' privacy is likely to lead to reprisals. Seeing the Good Folk when they didn't want you to is a good example of this. A woman from near Minehead in North Somerset accidentally saw twenty-four pixies at Great Gate on Exmoor. In revenge, they led her all night over the moor and through woods. Closely akin to this is the situation of midwives and wet nurses who, whilst in Faery to tend to children, are asked to anoint the infants with magical ointment which they then accidentally apply to their own eyes, dispelling the fairies' glamour and granting themselves the second sight, so that they can see faes even when they have assumed invisibility. These women are almost inevitably blinded for their presumption. Sometimes a faery will blow upon the enchanted eye, or touch it lightly with a finger; sometimes the response is far more brutal. A Guernsey fairy spat in a midwife's eye; a Welsh midwife had her eye rubbed, another was poked with a bulrush and a third girl had her eye pulled out whilst one Shetland midwife lost her vision by being poked with a long fingernail.[17]

Despite their mischievous nature, the faeries never respond well to tricks played against them. On a farm near Llanover, the custom was to leave the *tylwyth teg* bread and milk every night. One night, a bowl of urine was left out instead as a joke by one servant. The urine was thrown everywhere in the kitchen whilst the culprit was informed that there would always be an 'idiot' in his family. So it was that, in every generation, one person with mental disabilities was born as a reminder of the faeries' displeasure.[18]

17 F. Hancock, *Parish of Selworthy,* 1877, 248; W. Cob, 'Anglesey Folklore, *Y Cymmrodor,* vol.7, 1886, 197; Rhys, *Celtic Folklore,* 198, 213, 228, 247 & 248; *Glasgow Herald,* April 9th 1886, 10, '*Shetland Folklore.*'.
18 Rhys, *Celtic Folklore,* 193–194.

Trespassing on fairy ground is almost always treated as a gross violation of their rights. The fairies have been known (at the very least) to blunt farmers' scythes if they try to mow the grass growing on a fairy ring. Suspected witch Jonnet Miller, from Kirkcudbright, was a folk healer who diagnosed an illness caused by digging up a thorn tree, a very obvious example of faery revenge for a severe trespass against them. When a Scottish laird decided to evict the local fairies from their knoll at Blelack, a hill called the *Seeley Howe*, they cursed him, his heirs and his assistants with grief and loss – which duly fell upon them all – with the laird losing his estates in the 1745 rebellion. A second Scottish example comes from Caithness. In 1809 David Gunn of Houstry was making a new kitchen garden and he removed some stones for the wall from an ancient broch standing near to his cottage. He knew this was a fairy dwelling, but took the materials anyway. The fairies' revenge struck the whole community: a plague fell on the cattle of the entire district as a result. Somewhat comparable may be the story of the walnut tree that once grew at Llandyn Hall, Llangollen, around which the faeries met at night to hold their wedding ceremonies. When it was cut down in the nineteenth century, the faeries took their revenge, it was believed: one of the workmen involved in the felling was killed by a falling branch.[19]

Needless to say, stealing from the fairies tends to be harshly treated. A man from South Uist called Luran seems to have had a lucky escape. He entered a fairy knoll, sticking his knife in the threshold of the door so that it could not close forever behind him, and then stole a golden cup. As he fled the fairies called out "If porridge was Luran's food, he would catch the deer." Imprudently, perhaps, he took this as advice that would make

---

19 'Fairies, Egyptians and Elders,' Margo Todd, in Grell & Heal, *The Impact of the European Reformation,* 2008, 193; *Leeds Mercury,* May 13th 1882, 1 'Hazlethorpe Papers, Folklore – Fairies;' *Glasgow Herald,* August 15th 1896, 4 'St Wallach's Country;' R. Maclagan, 'Sacred Fire,' *Folklore,* vol.9, 1898, 280.

him even swifter and started to eat porridge as recommended. In fact, he put on weight and, when he rashly decided to make a return visit to the knoll, he was unable to outpace the fairies and was caught. Surprisingly, his captors settled for recovering their stolen cup and then let him go. There is one Welsh account, of the theft of quantities of gold and silver coins from the *tylwyth teg*, that ends with the culprit disappearing forever – allegedly executed by the faes. This reaction sounds rather more in character, to be sure.[20]

One particular intrusion upon their privacy, deliberately spying upon their activities, is especially enraging to faeries. Many reports of the fairies' vicious reactions to discovering that their private activities have been overlooked come from the Isle of Man. For example, some men riding home at night saw a light in an old kiln. One looked inside and saw a great crowd assembled but, almost instantly, the light went out and the witness was seized with sickness and found he could not walk. A similar Manx account ends even more unfortunately. Two men were walking home over the mountains when they passed an old, ruined cottage that was now just used as a cattle byre. However, on that night they heard music emanating from the house. The windows had been blocked up with turfs so one of the men peered through the keyhole of the door instead. He saw fairies dancing – but was seen himself almost immediately. The fiddler at the gathering jabbed the spy in his eye with the violin bow – and the man was blinded from that date.

Such reactions were by no means unique to the Manx fairies. A Hertfordshire folktale, *The Green Lady,* concerns a girl who set out to seek her fortune and is given work as a housemaid by the fairy woman of the title (the story bears close resemblances to the Cornish story *Cherry of Zennor*). The new maid is warned not to eat the food in the house and not to spy on the activities of her mistress. The girl proves too nosey though and (like the

---

20 *www.tobarandualchais.co.uk,* August 1957; Rhys, *Celtic Folklore,* 255.

Manx traveller) looks through the keyhole of one of the rooms on the woman's house. Inside, the Green Lady is dancing with a bogey – and the maid loses her sight for this violation (although in this story she is able to restore her vision with a magic well in the grounds of the property).

In the Scottish Highlands, near Braemar, there lies the Big Stone of Cluny. This has always been known to be a gathering place of the *sith* folk and, one night, a man saw a number of tiny figures dancing on top of the stone. He watched for some time, as his fancy was taken by one fairy girl in particular, but she sensed his presence and flew at him in fury. He only just had time to say a prayer and protect himself from what could have been permanent injury. At Beddgelert in Snowdonia, another man spied upon the fairies when they were dancing. This time, though, he fell asleep where he was concealed and, whilst he slumbered, was bound with ropes and covered with gossamer. Search parties who looked for him the next day couldn't see him and it was only the next night that the *tylwyth teg* freed him, after he had slept for a day and a half.[21]

I should add that trespasses against the faeries' moral code might be punished even where the victim was a human. For example, a man who had seduced a girl on Shetland was punished by the trows, who bound and carried him through the town where they both lived, exposing and shaming the abuser whilst an unfaithful wife from Tullibody near Stirling was carried off to the Fairy Knowe on the hill of Airthrey. In a comparable incident from Wales, a husband who treated his wife "harshly and unkindly" was snatched by the *tylwyth teg* and dropped in a lake. This highlights for us the fact that the faeries' violence might sometimes be inflicted with the aim of helping humankind.[22]

---

21 Rhys, *Celtic Folklore,* 104–105.
22 *www.tobarandualchais.co.uk,* Sept. 27th 1974; Fergusson, *Ochil Fairy Tales;* Rhys, *Celtic Folklore,* 54.

Verbal Assaults

Insults to fairies are very likely elicit a severe response: a drunken man on the Isle of Man met some fairies dancing at Laxey. He swore at them and they chased him away by pelting him with gravel. This wasn't sufficient though: soon his horse and cow died and, within six weeks, he died himself. In a story from Islay, a man in a pub one night toasted the local *cailleach* or hag in a mocking manner. She waylaid him on his way home and assaulted him. Not learning his lesson, he vowed vengeance for this and had a dagger made specially to defend himself when he saw her again. One day during harvest, though, the *cailleach* managed to get between him and where he'd put down the blade; she put her arms round his body and squeezed him until blood came out of his mouth.[23]

In the ballad of *Mary O'Craignethan,* the heroine is kidnapped by a "fairy wight" and her father curses them in response – "A malison braid on the fairy folk, Lie heavy late and air." He then threatens to fell all the trees where the fairies hold their court, although he is advised "dinnae curse the Seelie Court." Following an elaborate procedure, the father manages to retrieve Mary, but he soon dies, for "nane e'er curs'd the Seelie Court/And ever after thrave."[24]

Making light of faery help, and deprecating their generosity, seems to be regarded as insulting, as one man on Guernsey discovered. Out in a field ploughing one day, he heard voices call for a peel to get bread from a hot oven. He responded "we'll have cake soon," and then saw one lying on the ground nearby. Going to pick it up, he received a blow on his head.[25]

---

23 *Isle of Man Times,* April 24th 1889, 4 'Antique Mona;' J.G. Campbell, *Witchcraft & Second Sight,* 189.

24 'The Ballad of Mary O'Craignethan,' *Edinburgh Magazine & Literary Miscellany,* vol.83, 1819, 527.

25 M. de Garis, *Folklore of Guernsey,* 1975, 157.

Sometimes, again, what offends can be something a human does almost without thinking. The use of religious words and gestures in front of the faeries is a very good example of this. It may be an instinctive exclamation of 'Good god' or 'Bless me,' but it may equally be an action that can seem much more deliberate and antagonistic to fairy-kind. A district nurse called Pritchard was called at night to a woman in labour. Although the mother was a young girl, the rest of the family were "dwarfish people" and the nurse soon realised that she was dealing with a human abducted as a faery wife. Nurse Pritchard felt she ought to try to baptise the new born child and, for that matter, the mother, who had belonged to a Baptist congregation and had therefore not been baptised when she was taken by the faeries aged seven. The *tylwyth teg* quickly realised what was happening and expelled the nurse from their mound. Sometime later, she saw one of the 'dwarfish' men again; he shook his fist at her, shouted angrily in a strange language and then released a bull and a herd of cows to chase her down the road.[26]

Failing to be truthful with a fae seems to fall into this general category of offence. Lying to faeries is *never* advisable. A man from Osdale on Skye met a beautiful faery woman (although she was only three feet tall) and began a relationship with her. She promised to help him whenever he needed her assistance. He was, however, already married, an awkward fact he kept secret from her. In time, the man's wife became pregnant but her labour was very difficult and he feared for her life. He went to his faery lover and told her that one of his calving cows was ill. With the faery's help a son was safely delivered, but later she discovered the deception and in revenge took the baby away to live with her.[27]

---

26 D. Pugh Jones, 'A Case Not Entered,' *Welsh Outlook*, vol.18(2), Feb. 1931, 45.

27 Seton Gordon, *The Charm of Skye*, 125; see too B. Fairweather, *Folklore of Glencoe*, 1974, 3.

A jilted and betrayed faery lover can be an even more dangerous opponent. A Scottish man once had a *leannan sith* lover, but then married a mortal woman as well. She became pregnant but the birth was overdue. The man happened to meet his faery lover and she gave advice on speeding up the labour, but the man quickly realised that, in fact, she was trying to impede matters and to place a spell on his wife. He picked some of the special herb pearlwort (*mothan*), and put it in his wife's bed, after which the child was soon delivered.[28]

Physical Assaults

If the faes are upset by violations of their property, any sort of trespass against their persons is bound to attract reprisals. At Rudha Ban in Tarbet the wife of the head of the Macfarlane clan fell ill after the birth of a child and couldn't nurse her baby. Her husband decided to kidnap the wife of a local urisk and made her act as wet nurse. In revenge for this afront, the urisk mutilated the family's milkmaid. In turn, he was hanged.[29]

Any sort of assault giving rise to injury should plainly be avoided. A Norman knight who came upon fairies dancing at Beddgelert set his hounds upon the happy throng. His fate was first to get lost on his way back to his house. Then, when he managed to return home, he found his wife in the arms of her lover; the two men fought and the malicious knight died.[30] A more recent – and less elaborate – example of faery vengeance concerns a man called Gille Mor Dubh, who managed to capture the Lianachan *glaistig*. To get free, she promised to build him a house. He accepted, and the work was done in the blink of an eye. Once the work was completed, the *glaistig* offered to shake hands preparatory to going their separate ways. However, the

---

28 *www.tobarandualchais.co.uk,* March 1965.
29 Winchester, *Traditions of Arrochar and Tarbet,* 1916.
30 *Welsh Outlook,* no.11, Nov. 1st 1915, 431–2.

man had decided to trick the faery: he offered her not his hand but red-hot iron – which burned her severely. In response to this treachery, she cursed him. His new house burned down and all his family were dead within the year. In another version of this story, her vengeance was to call down monsters and the faery host (*an t-sluagh air*) upon him.[31]

Inevitably, reprisals will be taken for attempted murder. At Hawker's Cove, near Padstow, local man Tristram Bird discovered a mermaid one day whilst he was out hunting seals. She was sat on a rock, combing her hair and looking as alluring as mermaids can; he instantly desired her and asked her to marry him. She rejected the proposal and mocked him. He threatened to shoot her, and she warned him he'd be sorry if he did. He fired at her anyway – and regretted his action. When he shot at the mermaid, she cursed the harbour in response. Soon afterwards, a storm blew up – and a sandbar blocked all access from Padstow to the sea.

Some of these incidents are comprehensible, as acts of violence are met with violence. In some of the cases, though, the response seems disproportionate to the incitement – but no-one ever suggested that faeries are a proportionate people. I shall now concentrate upon two particular 'insults' to the faes – doubting their existence at all and violating the sanctity of their homes – both of which can give rise to notable animosity.

UNBELIEVERS

It definitely is not wise to doubt the existence of fairies – *and* to voice that disbelief too loudly or too forcefully. Here are a few examples of your likely fate if you do.

Denial in the face of tangible proof of the faeries' existence and capabilities is especially hated by them. Very common

---

31 *www.tobarandualchais.co.uk*, January 5th 1960; Seton Gordon, *Highways & Byways in the Central Highlands*, 1949, 173.

are stories of humans who win faery favour by mending their broken tools, and a regular element in these is the companion who doubts and mocks any such assistance. In a Sussex version of the story of the 'broken peel,' a ploughman mends the baking implement but his mate scorns the whole idea – and dies a year to the day later. In alternative versions, a gift of food is given in return for the repair and the companion refuses to eat it – and suffers as a result.

The *Leeds Mercury* for May 13th 1882 carried the story of an unbelieving butcher who was met one night by two female goblins. One jumped up behind him on his horse and the other ran alongside as he cantered along the road. He was so terrified by the experience that, as soon as he made it home, he went to bed and expired. Another sceptic went to a well-known haunt of a boggart and called out mockingly, asking where it was. It replied that it would be with him shortly, once its shoe had been tied, and, before he had a chance to think better of things and flee, it jumped out, grabbed him, and dragged him through bogs and briars until his clothes and skin were shredded and the pound of candles he had had in his pocket were reduced to the wicks alone. He was left in a ditch, barely more alive than dead.[32]

The pixies of the South West of Britain seem to be especially touchy about doubters and there are several stories of people punished by them for scepticism – usually by pixy-leading them. In William Bottrell's story of *Uter Bosence and the Piskey*, the man is drunkenly making his way home one night. He has laughed at stories of pixies and is regarded by other local people as an "unbelieving heathen" as a result. A fog arises and he becomes trapped in a field, unable to find the way out. Uter decides to rest in a ruined chapel until the weather improves – or dawn comes – but instead, he is confronted with a band of spriggans and a terrible goat-like being with blazing eyes and paws instead

32 'Hazelthorpe Papers – Folklore, Fairies,' *Leeds Mercury,* May 13th 1882, 1.

of hooves, which tries to dance with him. Then he's knocked over and dragged across the moor – an experience from which he never fully recovers.[33]

A Somerset man returning from the pub found himself misled and lost because he had sneered at the possibility of pixies. He was rescued by a local farmer who heard his cries of distress and, in response to the experience, the man undertook work on his saviour's farm for free, saying that he did this to please the pixies, so that they wouldn't give him a second "gude lammin'" the next time they came across him alone at night.[34]

In Enys Tregarthen's 1940 story, *Why Jan Pendogget Changed His Mind,* the main character is another disbeliever who unwisely is too vocal about his contempt for such childish ideas as pixies. He attends St Columb fair one day – and his mother advises him to avoid crossing Undertown Meadow on his way home because the pisky folk have been making rings there. Jan ignores this, of course, and is pixy-led. He can't find the gate out of the field and then can't locate the one he entered by either. He sees lights bobbing and hears the pixies laughing – and is trapped throughout the night until dawn sets him free.[35]

A Cornish miner called Tom Trevorrow doubted the existence of the knockers in mines. He refused to share his food with them and ignored the warnings of their displeasure at his disrespect (falls of stones in the workings), so finally they caused a roof collapse that buried the lode he had been working, along with all his tools.

One of the least violent of these types of tale may be the Dartmoor story of Nanny Norrish, whose scepticism is answered one night when she meets the pixies piled up before her in a pyramid and all chattering loudly. Nanny appears to have got

---

33 Bottrell, *Hearthside Tales,* vol.1, 57.
34 Mathews, *Tales of the Blackdown Borderland,* 58.
35 Tregarthen, *Folklore Tales,* 2020, 'Why Jen Pendogget Changed his Mind' (1940).

off lightly, considering what we've already seen and given that another Devon folklorist averred that the pixies' "malevolence will know no end" towards one who's spoken ill of them.[36]

The individuals described so far had a miserable time, wandering through bogs and bushes in the dark, but they got home eventually. Death may seem a disproportionate response to disbelief by the faeries, but it's not unheard of. A Shetland girl who had spoken lightly of the trows one night was drowned as she travelled home; a West Yorkshire man who mocked the boggarts instantly collapsed and died of a heart attack at Lumbutts, near Todmorden.[37]

RESPECTING FAERY HOMES

"Further, it is regarded as a distinct breach of elfin law or privilege to till fairy soil, or to remove stone, timber, or leaf from its precincts." No-one wants to see their home interfered with and, certainly, no right-minded person wants to damage a fairy's house. Unfortunately, given their habit of living under hills or even directly beneath human dwellings, the faeries are in a situation where their properties may easily be unwittingly damaged. The problem for the human who does this is that the consequences might be serious.[38]

Even quite minor trespasses appear to elicit very hostile responses. A man travelling over a hill near Loch Awe paused to rest at the summit, but two enraged faeries appeared. One wanted to throw him over a cliff, the other felt he should escape with a severe warning. The man was permitted to depart unscathed, but on a later occasion he passed the same way again and was roughly treated and bruised by three faeries,

---

36 Deane & Shaw, *Folklore of Cornwall,* 69; Crossing *Tales of Dartmoor Pixies* c.7.

37 J. Billingsley *West Yorkshire Folk Tales,* 2010, 41.

38 L. Spence, *British Fairy Origins,* 23.

who warned him never to return again on pain of even worse treatment. Usually, however, the reason for faery violence is more obvious, substantive and, even, understandable. For example, men building a new house on the Scottish island of Tiree took a stone from a nearby *sithean* or fairy hill. They had ample warning to desist as the stone kept returning nightly to the place where they found it – but they kept removing it again. Eventually, one of the builders fell ill, at which point they realised their error, reburied the stone and gave up.[39]

A comparable incident is reported from County Durham in Northern England. Soil was being dug from an old motte and bailey castle near Bishopton when a voice was heard to ask – "Is all well?" The excavators confirmed that it was, to which the voice replied "Then keep well when you're well and leave the Fairy Hill alone." This seems as unambiguous a warning as you could want – but in this case the men carried on digging regardless. Surprisingly, perhaps, they found a buried chest which, upon opening, was found to contain nothing but nails. No disaster followed, but we may be entitled to assume that there might have been gold had they paid more careful attention to the fairy words.[40]

An equally non-violent and yet compelling way of getting a human to remedy a trespass is seen in a case where a Scottish woman dreamed that she was visited by a strange female who complained that the stake for tethering a cow was letting rain fall onto her child's cradle. The first night this happened, the woman dismissed it. After the same dream three nights in a row, she realised that it was a message, so she went, closed up the hole she'd made – and ended the dream warnings.[41] In more common versions of this experience, the person who hammers

---

39 MacDougall & Calder, *Folk Tales and Faery Lore,* 191; *Celtic Magazine,* vol.8, 1883, 253.

40 Brockie, *Legends and Superstitions,* 83.

41 *www.tobarandualchais.co.uk,* Sept. 18th 1974.

a peg into a knoll to tether a horse is met with complaints from inside that he has made a hole that's now letting the rain in. He wisely and immediately agrees to tether his animal elsewhere; sometimes, in gratitude, the faes will direct him to the richest grazing nearby.[42]

The County Durham workmen just described seem very lucky when other examples are considered. An Orkney farmer who dug into a fairy mound was confronted by a little grey man who angrily told him that, if he took another spadeful, six of his cows would die and, if he still persisted, there would be six funerals in the family. Despite this very clear warning, the man went on with his work – with predictable results. In a comparable incident from Perthshire three men set out to strip turf from the top of a fairy hill. When they got there, they all felt suddenly exhausted and laid down for a nap. On awaking later, each had been carried off some distance, one finding himself a quarter of a mile away in a pool.[43]

Even disturbances in the vicinity of a fairy knoll can be fatal. On Islay it was decided to reclaim the waste land that surrounded a hillock called *Cnoc an-t Sithein* (Fairy Hill). It should probably have been pretty obvious that this land had been left fallow for a good reason; nonetheless, ploughing started. The first ploughman was killed by one of his horses in an accident soon afterwards. The next person set to the task was cursed with great bad luck.[44]

As the foregoing incidents all imply, the Scottish Highlands are dotted profusely with faery knolls, many of which mark the site of ancient brochs or duns. These places are well known to be faery locations and people are often reluctant at night to pass such 'Pict houses.' If a landowner wanted to excavate one, he had to be prepared to pay a hefty premium to his labourers to

---

42 Campbell, *Superstitions*, 93, 95 & 96.
43 Marwick 41; Murray no.85; Campbell, *Popular Tales*, 71 (no.3).
44 *www.tobarandualchais.co.uk*, 1970.

persuade them to undertake such inadvisable and dangerous work. A miller at Rosehall near Lairg in Sutherland dug earth from a knoll for his mill dam. The fairies responded instantly, swarming at him and driving him into the sea some twenty miles away before returning to destroy his new mill. This seems a relatively mild reaction compared to certain other cases. A farmer who completely destroyed a knoll was visited the same night by a mysterious little female who asked for 'a warming.' The man then found that, within only a couple of days, all his cattle started to die. What exactly this story means is made clear by the experience of another crofter who, in 1809, took stones from a broch to make a garden wall, and removed the earth to dress his vegetable plot. A small woman emerged from the hillock and warned that he'd have cause to repent, but imprudently he carried on. That night, a second small woman appeared in his home, warmed herself by his fire and advised him not to continue with his work on her home. The next day, he carried on regardless. During the next night, two of his cows died, followed by another two the succeeding day and so on. Worse still, the cattle plague spread to all his neighbours' herds too. In both these latter cases a communal ceremony had to be performed to end the pestilence. All the fires in the neighbourhood were extinguished and then relit from a single fire, through the smoke of which the surviving cattle were then driven. In a further version of this story from Skye, a man had destroyed the broch known as Dun Gharsain at Bracadale to get stones to build sheep pens. The *sith* swore vengeance, but were unable to harm him as he had been drinking milk from a cow grazed on the herb pearlwort or *mothan* (see later).[45]

Any ancient site may be associated with the faeries and, as such, should be approached with care. The dolmen at Vale on Guernsey called La Rocque qui Sonne was once threatened

---

45 Polson, *Our Highland Folklore Heritage*, 1926, 49, 50 & 133–135; *Carmina Gadelica*, vol.2, 308.

with destruction as a man tried to extend his house. The stones rang loudly as he started to break them up (hence the name of the monument) but he overlooked this clear warning. Within a year the new house had burned down, killing two maids. The householder tried to recoup some of the money he'd lost by selling some of the stones as building materials in England, but the ship carrying them sank. The man himself then moved to the island of Alderney, but his house there also burned down. All this misfortune was finally concluded when the culprit was on a ship at sea one day and the rigging fell onto his head, killing him. A related story concerns the dolmen at Rocquaine Bay on Guernsey. A man started digging there on the basis of rumours of buried treasure and, indeed, uncovered some pots filled with gold coins. However, as soon as he saw the hoard, it turned into limpet shells and a huge conger eel appeared which coiled itself around the pots. The man abandoned his work and fled, thereby avoiding further retribution.[46]

Fairy knolls really ought to be obvious places to avoid. Sometimes, it's much harder not to upset the faeries because their dwelling will be found directly beneath your own. John Rhys told the tale of a Gwynedd farmer who used to go outside his house to relieve himself every night before bed. One evening, a stranger appeared beside the man complaining about his annoying behaviour. The farmer asked how he could be upsetting a neighbour he'd never seen before, to which the stranger replied that his house was just below where they stood and, if the farmer placed his foot on the other's, he would see this. The farmer complied and with the transferred second sight saw clearly that all the slops from his house were going down the chimney of the other's home, which stood far below in a street he'd never seen before. The faery advised him to put his door in the other side of the house and that, if he did so, his cattle would never suffer from disease. The farmer obeyed

---

46 Marie de Garis, *Folklore of Guernsey*.

and after that time he was prosperous man. There are several versions of stories like this: in one, the grateful fairy later saves the householder's life.[47]

This proximity can clearly cause problems for the faery dwellers 'downstairs' but there can be inconvenience for the folk upstairs too. In one Scottish story a housewife was troubled by fairy women suddenly appearing at her cottage asking to borrow items or, unbidden, undertaking household tasks for her. On advice from a local wise man, the decision was made to demolish the house and rebuild it elsewhere. The thatch and rafters were, however, left behind and were burned after sprinkling nine dishes of sea water upon them. Later some men quarrying near the spot found bones buried, confirming for them that the place was frequented by ancestral spirits.[48]

The fairies in this last case seem to be *genii loci* – spirits of place. In another example, they almost seem to be part of the fabric of a building. Returning to the Scottish island of Tiree, the story is told of a house that was once plagued by fairies. They used to sit on the rafters in swarms and would sometimes drop down and steal a potato from the pot over the fire. Eventually, the tenant decided to move. He built a new home some distance away but, unluckily, ran out of materials before he'd finished. He took a stone from the old house to complete the job – which meant that the fairies came too.[49]

Fascinatingly, in this connection, Samuel Hitchins in his 1824 *History of Cornwall*, had this to say of fairy belief in the county. He felt that the fairy faith was fading, except amongst the aged and 'unenlightened' (in other words, amongst the gullible and ignorant – in his opinion), but still:

---

47 Marwick 35; Rhys 230
48 J.G. Campbell, *Waifs and Strays of Celtic tradition*, vol.IV, 83–86.
49 *Celtic Magazine*, vol.8, 1883, 253.

"By some, even the places of their resort are still pointed out, and particular fields and lanes are distinguished as spots which they were accustomed to frequent. To these bushes and hedges, near which they were presumed to assemble, some degrees of veneration are still attached. An indefinite species of sanctity is still associated with their beaten circles [fairy rings where they danced] and it is thought unlucky to injure their haunts or throw any obstacle in their way."

Hitchins noted as well that the historian William Borlase, in his *Antiquities*, had also observed how the Cornish still saw the spriggans and fairies as real beings in the landscape and paid them a kind of veneration. Hitchins may have been dismissive of such acts, but what's been described in this chapter may persuade readers that the older Cornish folk had good reason for their cautious respect.[50]

---

50 S. . Hitchins, *History of Cornwall,* 1824, vol.1, 97; Borlase, *Antiquities... of Cornwall,* 1758, 110.

CHAPTER FOUR

The Dangers of Faery Contact

Close contact with the faeries can lead to a variety of undesirable outcomes, both physical and mental. Some, arguably, are predictable. Given their amorous nature, and their strong attraction to humans, sexual assaults upon undefended females seem almost inevitable. Lewis Spence recorded that, for a "woman to sleep on a fairy hill or burial mound in the Highlands was to tempt conception from elfin sources." This is a very delicate way of describing sexual intercourse against their will whilst they slumbered. We know of similar cases of apparent opportunistic rape by selkies and testimony from at least one Scottish witch trial suggests that faery men were very prone to the sexual harassment of mortal women.[1]

Another direct – and mortal – threat comes from a number of female Highland faes. Kelpies are known for carrying off and devouring human victims, but in one story the creature transforms into an elderly woman who seeks a night's shelter in a shieling with a group of girls. They all share a single bed and one of the girls awakes during the night to find their visitor sucking the blood of her companions. Another alarming creature of this description is a class of 'green fairy woman' possessing bone beaks and cloven hooves who drink men's blood and

---

1 Spence, *British Fairy Origins*, 90; see the 1616 case of Elspeth Reoch, *Maitland Miscellany*, vol.2, part 1, 187–191 or of Katherine Jonesdochter, *Court Book of Shetland 1615–1629*, 1991, 39–40.

crunch up their skeletons. I shall return to these banshee monsters at the end of this chapter.[2]

Along the Scottish Borders with England, a couple of notably savage faery beings may be encountered. The Red Cap or Bloody Cap, has long teeth and talons and is armed with a pike. He haunts old ruins at night, lying in wait for travellers seeking shelter, whom he will murder. The malign goblin does this purely for the purpose of re-dyeing his headwear. Fortunately, he can be driven off by Christian symbols and will vanish with a flash of flame. The Powrie or Dunter, is another goblin that lives in old fortified towers. They make a beating noise that, if it gets louder, portends death and disaster – although it is not wholly clear whether it's Powrie who inflicts this.[3]

Other consequences of faery contact are less direct and far less expected. Examples of these follow in this chapter.

FAIRIES & DOGS

Fairies have a curious relationship to dogs. They have their own breeds, known as the *cu sith* in Scottish Gaelic, whilst, separately from this, some supernaturals appear in dog form – the black dogs and 'yeth hounds' of British folk tradition.[4] The faery relationship with dogs domesticated by humans is far less happy however.

Cu Sith

The fairy dogs of the Scottish Highlands are distinctive in appearance: they are the size of a young cow, green on their back and sides, with a tail that coils over their backs and paws the size of a man's hands. Their bark is very loud, capable of

---

2 Spence, *British Fairy Origins*, 92; J. McKay, 'Gaelic Folklore,' *Folklore*, vol.36, 169.

3 W. Henderson, *Folklore of the Northern Counties*, 1879, 215–218.

4 See my *Beyond Faery*, 2020, c.10.

scaring cattle to death, and they sound like horses galloping when they run. Although they can instil terror in a human, to the fairies themselves they are beloved household pets and guard dogs.[5]

Once some men on Barra were guarding their cows when they saw a large dog in the vicinity. Fearing for the herd's safety, they tried to strike the hound to scare it off (although one in the group suspected its true nature and warned against hurting it). The man who hit the dog was paralysed in his hand and arm and had to be carried home in great pain. A local wise woman diagnosed the fact that he was suffering fairy revenge and advised on a cure.[6]

Fairy dogs are expert hunters and one human who was favoured by two fairy women was given a fine specimen from which nothing ever escaped. This, of course, is a far less favourable trait where the prey is a human being and there are several versions of a story in which a woman forcibly retrieves a borrowed cooking pot from the local fairy knoll. The dogs are set on her and she is hard put to get home in one piece.[7]

Hair Off the Dog

There appears to be a strong antipathy between the dogs kept by humans and the faeries. It's not clear exactly why this should be so: sometimes the dog is protecting its owner, in other accounts it just seems to be drawn instinctively to chase and fight the supernatural being. Perhaps part of the dislike that is returned by the faeries is the fact that dogs seem, naturally, to be imbued with the second sight. In one story from Northumberland, for example, a man's dog would 'point' faeries, which were invisible to its master (although he could hear their music).[8]

5 Campbell, *Superstitions*, 141–144.
6 Campbell, *Popular Tales*, 47.
7 MacDougall & Calder, *Folk Tales*, 285.
8 Oliver, *Rambles in Northumberland*, 106.

Reasonable as this explanation sounds, there is one report that runs counter. It's said in the Highlands and islands of Scotland that the *sith* folk can induce female dogs and horses to attack their human owners. The way to render them harmless in such cases of 'fairy possession' is to either take blood from their ears or to collar them with a garter. Similar perhaps is the belief in the Outer Hebrides that you should never call your dogs by name at night, otherwise a *fuath* will come and summon both the hounds and the owner to follow it.[9]

Mostly, though, dogs will chase faeries or fight with them, even to the death. They seem to have an aversion to every type of supernatural and to be so provoked by their presence that they cannot be restrained. Fortunately for their own safety, the faeries seem to be able to thwart the dogs' ferocity by very simple means: Scottish folklorist J.G. Campbell tells a story about a dog called Luran who tried to stop the *sith* stealing his master's crops. The fairies got away, mockingly saying that he would have caught them if he'd been fed on porridge. The farmer heard this and changed his dog's diet. Still, he was defeated, because the hound liked the new food so much that he ate too much and was too full up to run – so that yet again the faes made their escape, laughing. A related story from Craignish has the escaping faery thieves scattering bread behind them, which the pursuing hound stops to gobble up.[10]

At Glenmoriston, near Loch Ness, there dwells a hag called the *Cailleach a' Craich*. She haunts a wild, high area where she will waylay and kill road users in a rather curious way (for details, see the end of this chapter). Having a dog as companion on the journey will protect the traveller, but the animal will be nearly flayed in the process and the owner will be left sick for months. In a related story (of which several variants survive) a man called Donald, son of Patrick, was sitting by his fire one

---

9   Campbell, *Witchcraft*, 184.
10 Campbell, *Superstitions*, 56.

night when a hideous hag asked for shelter. She was very large, with one huge tooth, and it was plain that, if he fell asleep, he would be doomed. Luckily, his hounds kept her at bay until dawn.[11]

The fairy female called the *glaistig* induces a similar response from hounds. A man called Ewan Cameron was crossing some hills at night and got lost. He saw a light in a hut and approached it, but inside there was a woman, drying herself by the fire and combing her hair. She asked him in to join her, but something warned him to decline. Her invitations got progressively more threatening and, eventually, he decided the only way he could escape was to set his four dogs upon her. He then managed to flee home. His three terriers were never seen again; only his greyhound returned to him and it was completely hairless. Two brothers from Onich, on Loch Linnhe, had a similar experience with a local *glaistig* who visited them whenever they were at a summer bothy. She was always troublesome on such visits and, one time, tried to grab one of the men. Their dogs defended them; one returned from its encounter with only a few tufts of hair on its ears and the other "was like a plucked hen." Comparable tales come from Arran, in which the dog saves its mistress from a hooved woman (very possibly a *glaistig*) and is mangled and scalped in the process, and from Mull. In this latter instance a young man called Callum was journeying at night when he was approached for a pinch of snuff by a small woman with no nostrils. He refused – and awoke the next morning to find that he'd slept out on the moors overnight and that his dog was bald.[12]

The bogies of the Highlands are likewise hated by dogs. In a story from the Isle of Mull, two men in a shieling hear a terrible screaming in the night, a bone-chilling sound that steadily draws

---

11 MacDonald, Gaelic Soc, vol.21 34; Campbell, *Superstitions*, 123.
12 Campbell, *Superstitions*, 32, 104 &145; MacDougall & Calder, *Folk Tales*, 243.

nearer to them. They go outside armed with sticks but can see nothing. A dark shape then passes them by and the sound fades. Their dog, however, makes chase and returns hairless – except for its ears. After the incident, the animal's coat never grew back properly – just a sort of down. On Islay a spectre called a *fuath* lurked in a notorious dell. One man's dog fought it, lost all its hair and soon expired. A *bocan* (or *baucan*) that haunted a lonely location on Arran could be kept at bay with a dog, too.[13]

The fearsome Highland water horse, the kelpie, that lived in the River Shin in the north west Highlands was also beaten and killed by a dog. However (as we're familiar with now) this victory was at the cost of the creature losing all its fur.[14]

Lastly, the fairies themselves might be savaged by hounds – and give as good as they got. Some men were minding the cow herds at Cornaigbeg on Tiree. They heard strange noises on the road, which made their dog very agitated. Something passed them by, sounding like the trampling of a herd of sheep (and which I assume to be the fairy host, the *sluagh*). Their dog pursued the noise, but returned with all its hair scraped off and its skin bare and white, except for a few torn and bloody spots. It died very soon afterwards. Another man out hunting on the same island encountered a fairy. He was so terrified that he fled immediately, leaving his dog behind in his confusion. The dog returned home to its master the next day, carrying the man's gun in its mouth. Yet again, it was left entirely hairless. In a related incident on Mull, a man travelling after midnight saw a light up in the hills and heard music. His dog raced off towards the apparition and the traveller continued alone to his destination, where he arrived, too scared to eat. Within a short while the dog turned up, but (as ever) it was completely hairless. It lay down at his feet and promptly died. On Arran, the story is told

---

13 Campbell, *Superstitions*, 144; Campbell, Witchcraft, 189; Mackenzie, *Arran*, 273.
14 Dempster, Folklore of Sutherlandshire, 223.

of a piper who descended into the King's Caves with his dog. It seems that he must have encountered the fairies there and was overcome: he never returned, although the dog did, completely bald.[15]

Finally, a farmer called Watson of Peelwyke near Keswick in the Lake District once saw two tiny people dressed in green in a meadow near his farm. Unwisely, we might think, he turned his dog loose on the pair. The dog set off fiercely enough, but almost straight away began to roll over and over in agony. The fairy couple, meanwhile, vanished.[16]

Summary

It's not wholly clear why encounters with faeries have such a drastic effect on dogs. Probably the loss of the entire coat is indicative of the violence of the encounter between two dimensions and the struggle of the faithful mortal pet against the malign supernatural forces. However, a version of the Arran piper story found on Skye, in which the musician enters the Golden Cave at Trotternish, has the dog return without its master and with its hair singed off by the fire and brimstone which the pair encountered underground. Here, of course, the subterranean fairies are becoming confounded with the devil – a fairly common occurrence. Very similar is a tale about Macphie of Colonsay, who was overtaken by night when he was out hunting and was forced to take shelter in a deserted hut. A dark banshee then tried to get in and his dog attacked her. After a while, the hound's fur started to smoke, a sign to Macphie to make his escape.[17]

In fact, there is some indication that it is not just dogs who may suffer in this manner. From Shetland come two stories of

---

15 *www.tobarandualchais.co.uk*, December 8th 1980; Campbell, *Superstitions*, 145.

16 W. Dickinson, *Cumbriana: Fragments of Cumbrian Life*, 1876, 131.

17 Campbell, *Superstitions*, 118.

children made bald by encounters with the trows. In the first, a small boy went missing in the vicinity of his home. His mother searched for him in a panic, calling his name, and she heard him reply that he was on an old trow woman's back – obviously in the process of being carried off to the grey folk's hill. The trow dropped the boy at this, but gave him a slap on his head that left him bald for the rest of his life. In another incident, a 'clout on the croon' left a similar bald patch on the child's head.[18]

Whatever the exact explanation of these accounts, their consistency only serves to stress to us the dangerous nature of any such meetings.

'LET ME GRAB YOUR SOUL AWAY' – ABDUCTING SPIRITS

An account of folk beliefs in North East Scotland, includes this fascinating note:

> "It is said that, if a person dies of consumption, the fairies steal the soul from the body and animate another person with it."[19]

Sir Walter Scott confirmed this tradition from a manuscript history of Moray that he possessed, recording that "in a consumptive disease, the fairies steal away the soul and put the soul of a fairy in the room of it." This sounds rather more like a changeling substitution than an abduction, but the cure involved passing the afflicted person three times through a wreath of oak and ivy (not a practice known in changeling cases).[20]

In the far north of Scotland, then, fairy abductions of humans can include not just a physical kidnapping of an individual but

---

18 *Old Lore Miscellany, Orkney and Shetland,* vol.2, 1908, 109.
19 Shaw, *The History of the Province of Moray,* 1827, 278.
20 W. Scott, *Minstrelsy,* VI.

the abstraction of a person's vital essence, leaving an inanimate stock behind: their soul is in Faery and a lifeless shell remains in the mortal world with their family and friends. Related to this may be the Shetland belief that trows can only appear in human form if they can find someone who's not been protected by a 'saining' or blessing. In accordance with this idea, there is one story in which two trows attend a Yule dance in the form of two small boys whose mother had forgotten to bless them before she went out for the night's festivities. When they were exposed the trows vanished from the dance, but the boys didn't return to their beds. They were found the next day, lying dead in a deep snowdrift. Fairy 'possession' can lead to real or simulated death, therefore, as well as following on from it.

In the Hebrides, an identical belief to that seen in the north east once prevailed. If a person is slowly dying of consumption, the faeries will be watching to steal the sufferer's soul, so that it can be used to give life to another body. The practice to protect the person in such circumstances was to cut their nails, tie up the clippings in a rag, and to wave this three times in a clockwise direction around their head.[21]

A final example of soul taking comes from Sutherland and relates to the *sluagh,* the fairy host. Stories of people physically carried away through the air by the host are quite common, but the fairies need not take the body. One man who regularly travelled at night with the faes was forcibly restrained by friends and family, but the fairies were still able to take his spirit with them on their journeys.[22]

Faeries & the Dead

These particular Scottish manifestations may be unique, but the idea that faeries (or, at least, some of them) have some

---

21 Gordon Cumming, *In the Hebrides,* 1883, 267.
22 Mackay, 'Fairies in Sutherland,' *Celtic Magazine,* vol.9, 1884, 207.

association with the souls of the dead is widespread in the British Isles. The pixies of the south-west might be the souls of unbaptised children, or those delivered stillborn, or perhaps the spirits of virtuous druids and other non-Christians. The mine sprites (the 'knockers') were said to be the souls of ancient miners and there are also traces of a belief that bees and moths were spirits in some form. In Wales, as well, the *tylwyth teg* were thought to be the spirits of virtuous druids who had died in pre-Christian times, whilst on the Isle of Man the belief was that the little folk represented the souls of those who died before the Flood.[23]

In Yorkshire, the supernatural hounds called the Gabriel Ratchets were believed to be the form taken by infants who died before baptism; they would return to circle their parents' home overhead at night. Other 'fairy beasts' such as the black dogs, shugs and shocks were regarded as portents of death in the counties where they were seen. The Welsh equivalent of these hounds, called the *Cwn Annwn* (roughly, the hounds of hell) were ban dogs employed for the pursuit of the souls of those who had died either unbaptised or unshriven. On Guernsey, the subterranean faeries appear to people at night as black dogs or as goats with fiery eyes, prompting folklore writer Marie de Garis to class them as spirits of the dead.[24]

Certain people – those who died early, unexpectedly or by violence – would go to live with the fairies in a sort of limbo. This is a concept found across Britain in folklore, ballad and poetry from at least the Middle Ages. The idea is laid out very clearly in the poem *Sir Orfeo:*

> "Þan he gan bihold about al
> Ond seiȝe [saw] ful liggeand wiþin þe wal
> Of folk þat were þider ybrouȝt
> Ond þouȝt dede, ond nare nouȝt.
> Sum stode wiþouten hade

---

23 Evans Wentz, *Fairy Faith*, 183, 169, 179, 177, 178, 147 & 123.
24 See my *Beyond Faery*, 2020, c.10; de Garis, *Folklore of Guernsey*, 1975, 154.

Ond sum non armes nade
Ond sum þurth þe bodi hadde wounde
Ond sum lay wode [mad], ybounde,
Ond sum armed on hors sete
Ond sum astrangled as þai ete
Ond sum were in water adreynt
Ond sum wiþ fire al forschreynt;
Wives þer lay on childbedde,
Sum ded, ond sum awedde [mad];
Ond wonder fele þer lay bisides
Riȝt as þai slepe her undertides.
Eche was þus in þis warld ynome,
Wiþ fairi þider ycome."

All the people seen within the walls of the faery king's castle had been taken before their time from the world – by drowning, choking, in childbirth or by murder – and had been carried off to faeryland. It is, perhaps, particularly notable that individuals considered to have gone mad – to have lost their wits, we might say – had in reality been abstracted by the faes.

A remarkably similar scene is to be found in the Cornish faery story *Cherry of Zennor.* The heroine is given a job as a nurse maid by a mysterious widower and goes to live in his strange house.

"After a few days, old Aunt Prudence took Cherry into those parts of the house which she had never seen... they entered a room, the floor of which was like glass, and all round, perched on the shelves, and on the floor, were people, big and small, turned to stone. Of some, there were only the head and shoulders, the arms being cut off; others were perfect. Cherry [had] thought from the first she was got into a land of Small People underground, only her master was like other men; but now she know'd she was with the conjurers, who had turned all these people to stone.

Old Prudence laughed at Cherry, and drove her on, insisted upon her rubbing up a box, 'like a coffin on six legs,' until she could see her face in it. Well, Cherry did not want for courage, so she began to rub with a will; the old woman standing by, knitting all the time, calling out every now and then: "Rub! rub! rub! Harder and faster!" At length Cherry got desperate, and giving a violent rub at one of the corners, she nearly upset the box. When, O Lord! it gave out such a doleful, unearthly sound, that Cherry thought all the stone people were coming to life, and with her fright she fell down in a fit..."

Later Cherry spies on her master in the room by looking through the key-hole and sees him with lots of ladies, singing, while one dressed like a queen is playing on the coffin.[25]

Sir Walter Scott later used this same idea in his ballad 'Alice Brand,' which is incorporated into his 1810 poem *The Lady of the Lake*. Alice and her lover Richard are hiding in the greenwood; the Elfin King hears them cutting down his trees and sends a goblin to chastise them:

"Up, Urgan, up! to yon mortal hie,
For thou wert christen'd man:
For cross or sign thou wilt not fly,
For mutter'd word or ban."

When the goblin finds the pair, Alice confronts him and asks how he fell under the king's power. He replies:

"It was between the night and day,
When the Fairy King has power,
That I sunk down in a sinful fray,
And 'twixt life and death, was snatch'd away
To the joyless Elfin bower."

25 Robert Hunt, *Popular Romances of the West of England*, vol.1, 118.

Alice is then able to release from this captive state by making the sign of the cross three times.[26]

What appeared so frequently in verse and story merely reflected genuine folk belief, as is confirmed by the evidence given by several Scottish witchcraft suspects. In addition, in folk accounts of those visiting faery, perhaps as musicians or as guests, it is not uncommon to hear that they recognise some of those in the company as being deceased neighbours. More specifically, for example, Alisoun Peirson told her inquisitors that several deceased members of her family were to be found in the court of Elphame, including her uncle William Simpson; Andro Man claimed in 1598 that he knew "sindrie dead men in thair cumpanie" (one of whom was the late King James IV, who had been killed at the Battle of Flodden in 1513). Bessy Dunlop revealed that the laird of Auchenreath, who had died nine years previously, was to be seen amongst the fairy rade whilst her particular 'familiar,' a man called Thom Reid, had fallen at the battle of Pinkie some twenty-nine years earlier. Elspeth Reoch's fairy intermediary was a relative called John Stewart, who had been murdered at sunset – a violent and premature death at a liminal time of day.

Scottish folklorist John Francis Campbell collected a number of stories that showed how, "according to popular belief, fairies commonly carry off men, women and children who seemed to die, but really lived underground. In short, that mortals were separated from fairies by a very narrow line." Another writer on Highland folklore, Canon John Arnott MacCulloch, neatly summarised these folk beliefs as follows: "Popular tradition does actually regard certain fairies as souls of the dead, *or rather of certain classes of dead persons...*" (my emphasis).[27]

Lewis Spence surveyed the wider thought behind these folklore traditions in his classic *British Fairy Origins*. He noted,

---

26 *Sir Orfeo; Fairy Dwelling on Silena Moor; 'The Tacksman of Auchriachan.'*
27 Campbell, *Popular Tales*, vol.2, 76; J.A. MacCulloch, 'Were fairies an earlier race of men?' *Folklore*, vol.43, 365.

for example, that the soul is often conceived as being a small person and that it is easy to understand how the little folk and the spirit homunculus might become confused. He also pointed to the very common fact that, across Britain, faeries are found living in ancient burial mounds. Spence's summary of the evidence was that "a greater number of resemblances seem to exist between the dead and fairies than differences divide them." Thus, "it is not possible to regard fairy spirits in general as other than spirits of the dead…"[28]

Walter Evans-Wentz, in *The Fairy Faith in Celtic Countries*, also espoused the theory that (some at least of) the fairies are the souls of the dead, something which he set within a pan-Celtic 'Legend of the Dead.' He said that:

> "the striking likenesses constantly appearing in our evidence between the ordinary apparitional fairies and the ghosts of the dead show that there is often no essential and sometimes no distinguishable difference between these two orders of beings, nor between the world of the dead and fairyland."[29]

The Reverend Robert Kirk in the *Secret Commonwealth* even went so far as to argue that, whilst the bodies of the dead lie in their graves in the churchyard, their souls inhabit the fairy knowes that are so often found in proximity to Highland churches. He confirmed that faeries were, therefore, believed by some with the second sight to be "departed souls, attending awhile in this inferior state, and clothed with Bodies procured through their Almsdeeds in this Lyfe… but if any were so impious as to have given no Alms, they say when the Souls of such do depart, they sleep in an unactive state till they resume the terrestrial Bodies again." Other seers believed that the souls of the dying

---

28 Spence, *British Fairy Origins*, c.4, especially 68, 70, 80 & 83.
29 Evans Wentz, *Fairy Faith*, 280 & 493.

people became wraiths, or the apparitions of black dogs which I mentioned earlier, whilst yet others were convinced that the fairies were "a numerous People by themselves, having their own polities." Kirk mentioned too other beliefs that people's "Souls goe to the *Sith* when dislodged" and that some will "go to the *Siths* (or People at Rest, and in respect of us, in Peace) before the natural Period of their Lyfe expire..." These concepts seem very clearly to be identical with the idea that those murdered or otherwise killed violently end up in faery. Seventeenth century Scottish opinion on the nature of fairykind was divided then, but it was apparently as common to see them as some manifestation of human dead as it was to consider them to be a separate form of life.[30]

Scots poet Robert Sempill put these ideas into verse, describing how one suspected witch:

> "names our nyboris sex or sewin [six or seven],
> That we belevit had bene in heawin."[31]

That those taken into the faery hill only appear to have died is demonstrated in a number of Scottish stories in which the deceased person returns to a spouse or lover to explain their predicament and to seek help. This often happens in dreams, although a ghost-like apparition might also be seen. If the right steps are then taken, the individual will be able to return and often then will reveal that what had been buried was not their corpse at all, but a stick or log of alder wood. Sometimes these pleas to the survivors for redemption fail because the living fear to restore the 'dead' to life.[32]

---

30 *Secret Commonwealth*, chapters 7 & 10; 'Tarbott's Relation' sections 3 & 10. NB: underlying Kirk's later comments is the fact that *sith* in Gaelic can mean both 'peace' and the 'knolls,' the faery hills, as well as – by extension – their inhabitants.
31 *The Legende of the Bischop of St Androis Lyfe.*
32 Campbell, *Superstitions,* 83, 86–87 & 89.

THE DANGERS OF FAERY CONTACT

Back to Life?

Those humans residing with the faeries may very well have been taken there against their wills: many are deprived of their mortal, earthly lives suddenly and at a young age. They are not old, ill and content to die, but are snatched in the prime of life and are very likely to be resentful at their abductions.

This leads us to the issue of escape from Faery. In the traditional accounts, we often come across individuals who wish to return home but find themselves unable to do so for a variety of reasons. They may be magically trapped in the performance of Sisyphean tasks that can never be completed, baking bread from inexhaustible supplies of flour and the like, or they may find that by partaking of faery food and drink, they have acquired faery nature and, as such, cannot depart. A Manx visitor inside a faery palace was advised by one of the revellers not to drink the wine he was offered unless "he wished to be as they were and return no more to his family."[33] What's implicit here is that some physical change has occurred which cannot be reversed; the proof of this comes from stories such as that of *King Herla*. After attending the fairy king's wedding, the king and his company return to their world, but find that many ages have passed and that they cannot dismount from their horses without crumbling away into dust. They are left to ride unceasingly and forever, thereby connecting us back to ideas of the 'wild hunt' and the yeth hounds mentioned earlier, endlessly riding in pursuit of lost souls. Any attempted escape from Faery is likely to be attended by disappointment and unhappiness, which leads us to our next subject – the psychological impact of fae contacts.

MENTAL EFFECTS

Today many people are determined to believe that contact with faes represents blessing and felicity, but the folklore record often

---

33 G. Waldron, *Description of the Isle of Man,* 1728, 28.

reveals that contact with the faeries for any period of time can have an adverse effect upon a human being. Whether this is the consequence of mere proximity to them, or whether it is the result of being exposed to their different world, is a good deal less clear, but the personal consequences are very distinct. In *British Fairy Origins,* Lewis Spence commented how a kidnapped adult, upon returning to his home and acquaintances, "almost inevitably found it impossible to adjust himself to mortal ways and generally succumbed to the allurements of the fairy mound."[34]

The joys of life with the faeries certainly seem to be part of the process by which humans are abducted, as a story from Morvern, south west of Fort William, demonstrates. A local man whose wife had recently given birth had to go out one day. However, he left a group of women watching over his wife and baby and was not concerned. On returning at night, he found that the fire gone out and the women were all fast asleep. He rekindled the fire in the hearth, only to look up to see a *bean sith* entering the room and making for the bed where his wife and child were. The man took a faggot from the fire and threw it at her. A flame gleamed about his eyes for an instant and the *bean sith* vanished. When she awoke, his wife declared that she felt at the time like one in a nightmare (*trom-a-lidhe*); she had heard voices calling upon her to go out, and felt an irresistible inclination to obey them.[35]

There are numerous folklore accounts of the impact of being separated from the faery presence. For example, one of the best pipers in Sutherland was taken by the faeries to play at their feasts and celebrations. After several years' absence, a midwife who had been called to a birth in the fairy knoll spotted the man there and told him of all the changes that had taken place in his absence. He couldn't believe what she was saying, because he

34 Spence, *British Fairy Origins,* 41.
35 Campbell, *Superstitions,* 80–81.

was convinced that he'd been there only a few minutes. He was eventually freed from the faeries, but when he got home, he was very weak and hardly seemed to recognise his old friends and family. In fact, he didn't even want to associate with them any longer. The piper didn't seem to belong in his old world anymore and, after a while, he took his bagpipes and disappeared back to the fairy knoll. A man from Skye who had taken a faery lover suffered in an identical manner. He was left unable to settle in his old life with his wife and family, ultimately wandering away and abandoning them.[36]

A boy from Skye who joined a faery dance in the dun of Torvaig, at Scorrybreck, was thought by his family to be dead, but he came back home after three weeks. Sadly, though, he was "never the same lad; for he was ever distraught in manner and ever sighing for the joys of the fairy-haunted dun."[37]

On Shetland it is said that, if a person becomes melancholy and low spirited, this is because the trows have stolen the real person and have left behind a "moving phantom" in his or her stead. Alternatively, the heart has been stolen, the cure for which is the ceremony of 'casting the heart,' which I describe in detail later.[38]

Very similar, perhaps, is the fate of a Glamorgan man who danced with the *tylwyth teg*. He thought he had been with them only five minutes when he was rescued a year later. After his return to the mortal world, he was struck with a "melancholy madness" and died within a short time. Time spent in Faery can be joyous, therefore, but it can be shattering.[39]

---

36 Polson, *Our Highland Folklore Heritage*, 57–58; Seton-Gordon, *The Charm of Skye*, 1929, 231.

37 'Folklore of Skye,' *Folklore*, vol.33, 202.

38 Anon, 'Extracts from a Journal Kept During a Coasting Voyage Through the Scottish Islands,' *Edinburgh Annual Review*, vol.5(2), 1812, 434; Gomme, 'Trows of Shetland,' *Gentleman's Magazine Library*, 1885, 51.

39 *Cardiff Times*, September 15th 1888, 1 – 'Welsh Gleanings.'

Leading Scottish authority John Gregorson Campbell provided us with a very different interpretation of the same phenomenon:

> "... the man is greatly to be pitied whom the elves get power over, so that he exchanges his human lot and labour for their society or pleasures. Wise people recommend that, in the circumstances, a man should not utter a word till he comes out again, nor, on any account, taste fairy food or drink. If he abstains, he is very likely before long dismissed, but if he indulges, he straightway loses the will and power ever to return to the society of men. He becomes insensible to the passage of time, and may stay, without knowing it, for years, and even ages, in the brugh. Many, who thus forget themselves, are among the fairies to this day. Should they ever again return to the open air, and their enchantment be broken, the fairy grandeur and pleasure prove an empty show, worthless, and fraught with danger. The food becomes disgusting refuse, and the pleasures a shocking waste of time."[40]

For Campbell, the mental impact of leaving Faery was not the shock of being deprived of their eternal pleasures, but the appalling realisation that they were all illusion. However, we may wish to diagnose the cause, though, the result is the same: the person returning to the mortal world is destabilised and unhappy.

SPEECHLESS

We expect to be able to communicate with our Good Neighbours and, most of the time, this happens without comment. From time to time, however, the incomprehensibility of the fairy

---

40 Campbell, *Superstitions*, 17.

tongue is remarked upon. We may draw several conclusions from this: either that they share – and have always shared – our speech with us, or that close proximity with us over centuries has made them bilingual – even though they may naturally, amongst themselves, speak another language entirely. According to one Scottish witch suspect, Anne Cairns (tried and executed at Dumfries in April 1659), the 'fferie' were "not earthen folkis" and spoke "no earthly talkis" but rather conversed with "ane eldridge voyce."

However, what we also find is that contact with the fairies can require – or lead to – loss of a human's voice. One interpretation of the Gaelic term *sith* is that it signifies the peaceful or silent nature of the faes. "The fairies come and go with noiseless steps and their thefts or abductions are done silently and unawares to men." From this perspective, silence may be the result of being near the fays or it is the price of being in their company – the safest option when they are near. For example, sometime in the early nineteenth century a young farmer called Owen employed a labourer who had constant dealings with the *tylwyth teg*. One time the employee took his master with him to visit a faery house. The pair were given animals to ride home, the labourer on a donkey and Owen on a large calf. The latter was told *not* to speak when crossing a river but he did do so – and was thrown off into the water. Another encounter with the *tylwyth teg*, which took place at Gors Goch near Lampeter, also led to a loss of speech. The fair family entered a house wanting to bathe and dress their children there. They woke the inhabitants, demanding fresh water, but at first none of the human family were able to speak or to move. Finally, a Breadalbane man who was roughly carried off from his garden by a host of faeries returned home with his hair in elf-knots and deprived of the power of speech.[41]

---

41 Campbell, *Superstitions*, 3; W. Cobb, 'Anglesey Folklore,' *Y Cymmrodor*, vol.7, 1886, 115; Rhys *Celtic Folklore*, 110; Pennant, *Tour of Scotland*, vol.1, 110.

It follows that intimate contact with a faery may well result in dumbness. At some time in the late eighteenth century, a native of Cornaig in Tiree was out shooting on the island and, returning home in the evening, he met a faery woman beside the stream that runs into Balefetrish Bay, near Kennovay. At first, he didn't notice anything in her appearance different from other women, but, when she leaned over the stream and kissed him, he saw she had only one nostril. On reaching home he found he was unable to articulate a single word. On the advice of a wise old man, the hunter composed, in his mind, a love song to the *bean sith*. On doing this, his speech was restored. A curious reversal of this incident is found in the Welsh story of Einion and Olwen. Shepherd boy Einion was led into Faery by an odd little man and was invited to dine with him and his family. He found himself unable to speak at first – that is, until Olwen kissed him.[42]

The importance of keeping silent in the presence of the faes is apparent in the faerylore from an early date. In the poem *Huon of Bordeaux*, the hero is advised "on jeopardie of losing your life, that you speake to [King Oberon] no word, without you purpose ever to abide with him." Just like eating faery food, it seems, conversation will curse the human speaker to remaining perpetually. Similarly, Thomas of Erceldoune is warned by his lover the fairy queen "whatso any man to thee say/Luke thou answer none bot mee." In this case, part of the need for caution is that the king might not have been happy to learn that Thomas had seduced his wife, but the need for reticence and silence in Faery is also apparent. Careless words can trap a human in Faery for ever.[43]

Elspeth Reoch was a young Orkney woman tried for witchcraft in March 1616. She told her prosecutors that she had been in contact with the fairies on and off since she was twelve years old. There is much that is interesting in her

---

42 Campbell, *Superstitions*, 109; Rhys *Celtic Folklore*, 112–113.
43 *Huon of Bordeaux*, c.21; *Thomas of Erceldoune*, stanza 41.

confessions, but here we are interested solely in the fact that she lost her voice after she had sex with one of two fairy men who approached her; this dumbness was to protect her against people's questions as to how she had gained the second sight. Elspeth lay with the man and, when she woke the next morning, she had "no power of her toung and could not speik."[44]

In her book, *Troublesome Things*, Diane Purkiss provides a full account of the case, along with considerable sociological and psychological theorising about Elspeth's situation. It looks as though Elspeth derived some income from begging as a mute and from telling fortunes, but that her own family were angry about her silence and allowed her brother to beat her quite severely to try to get her to speak. Purkiss' speculations over gender roles and power may be justified, but let's put Elspeth's loss of voice in a wider context of faery contacts, which suggests other interpretations of the victim's silence.[45]

Barbara Bowndie of Kirkwall was taken by the fairies for a day. She told her trial in 1644 that this experience had left her speechless for twenty-four hours – as well it might. Jonet Morrison, a suspect witch from Bute, told her trial in 1662 that she had healed a girl who had been blasted by the 'faryes.' The child, daughter of a man called McPherson, had been lying "without power of hand or foot and speechless" when Jonet's help was sought. She had made her well with herbs. In both these cases, loss of use of the tongue is the consequence of fairy proximity – whether deliberately inflicted or not.[46]

Speechlessness might be inflicted by indirect fairy power, too: it was alleged that Elgin woman, Janet Cowie, who had been taken by the fairies to their hill at Messindiu, had struck one woman dumb and had made another unable to walk for nine weeks. In fairness, the rest of the evidence against Janet was

---

44 *Maitland Miscellany*, vol.2, part 1, 187–191.
45 Purkiss, *Troublesome Things*, 2000, 90–96.
46 McPhail, *Highland Papers*, vol.3, 20–28.

that she was often out all night and would be seen lying half dead around the town or begging for money for alcohol. This very much sounds like a woman with a serious drink problem, rather than a malign sorceress, so we may be relieved to hear that she broke her bail and escaped her accusers (and almost certain death).[47]

John Stewart, tried for sorcery at Irvine in 1618, had acquired knowledge of palmistry from the fairies whilst in Ireland. One Halloween, he had met the king of faery and his court. The king had touched John on his forehead with his staff (wand), which had the effect of blinding him in one eye and making him dumb. Three years later John met the king again one Halloween and his sight and speech were restored. Stewart then met the fays regularly and acquired his skills from them. Very similar was the case of John Gothray, who told his 1640 trial before Perth presbytery that he had been abducted by the fairies and had stayed some time with them, in the care of his changeling brother, before being released endowed with healing powers but "distracted of his wits and speechless."[48]

Silence might also be enjoined upon a person when meeting the fays. The Reverend Robert Kirk stated that the "subterraneans [would] practice sleights for procuring a privacy to any of their mysteries." Any humans who had spent time with the faes under the hill might be "smit... without pain as with a puff of wind... or they strick them dumb." Bessie Dunlop is a very famous witch suspect, tried at Lyne in 1576. Once again, her confessions are a rich and fascinating source, but I am interested here only in one aspect. A fairy man (or ghost) called Thom Read was her supernatural adviser, helping her with cures for sick people and cattle and assisting her in the location of lost and stolen goods.

---

47 *Records of Elgin,* vol.2, 356 – November 26th 1646.

48 *The trial, confession & execution of Isobell Inch, John Stewart, Margaret Barclay & Isobell Crawford for witchcraft, 1618, at Irvine; RPC* vol.2; Gothray case in 'Fairies, Egyptians and Elders,' Margo Todd, in Grell & Heal, *The Impact of the European Reformation,* 2008, c.9.

On one occasion, Thom introduced Dunlop to twelve handsome fairy folk but, before they met, Thom forbade her to speak to them. The 'guid wichtis,' as Bessie called them, greeted her and invited her to go with them to Faery/Elfame. As instructed, she did not reply to this and they then conferred amongst themselves – although she couldn't tell or hear what they said, "onlie sche saw thair lippis move." This suggests that they were audible when addressing her directly but when speaking privately amongst themselves they were inaudible, whether that was deliberate or just a feature of fairy speech.[49] It's worth pointing out here that in several modern cases witnesses have reported an identical experience: they see the fays speaking but they hear nothing.[50] In this connection too, we might note the scattered but consistent reports on telepathic communication, in which the barriers of the spoken word are overcome entirely.[51]

Returning to the older faery encounters, silence might be enjoined not only to keep the human safe but to ensure a successful outcome. A woman of Rousay in Orkney, whose child had been taken by the trows, was instructed how to recover her infant by force. She had to break into the fairy lair, snatch back her baby and hit the fairy woman who'd abducted it with a bible, three times. Throughout this encounter, not a word was to be spoken, otherwise the rescue would fail.[52]

On other occasions Bessie Dunlop saw Thom Read in public, in the street and in the churchyard, but she was instructed on such occasions not to speak to him unless he spoke to her first. This may have been as much to do with concealment as with matters of confidentiality or communication between dimensions. Discretion over one's dealings with the fairies is always recommended: if they favour you with gifts of money –

---

49 Pitcairn, *Ancient Criminal Trials*, vol.1, 49–58.
50 For example, see Marjorie Johnson, *Seeing Fairies*, 48, 89 & 299.
51 Johnson 20, 80, 89, 111, 163 & 262.
52 Marwick, *The Folklore of Orkney* 83.

keep them secret or your good fortune will instantly be lost. In the same way, an Argyllshire woman who was abducted for two months by the 'wee folk' before managing to escape back to her husband and family ever afterwards maintained a complete silence about what she'd seen and done during her weeks away 'under the hill' in Faery. This respectful avoidance of gossip is highly advisable wherever our Good Neighbours are concerned.[53]

Lastly, the fairies could also help with curing loss of speech. Jonnet Miller of Kirkcudbright, tried for witchcraft in May 1658, was a folk healer who diagnosed and treated a man whose tongue had been 'taken' by the fairies. She advised him to cure himself using foxglove leaves and water taken from a south-running stream. As I'll discuss later, silence in collecting water from springs could often be an important part of the curing ritual. As an immediate example, Catie Watson of Stow was asked in about 1630 to treat a child that had been 'blasted' by the fairies. She instructed the mother to bring the sickly infant to her before sunrise, saying no words. During the 1560s Jennet Pereson of Wallsend was accused of witchcraft for treating a child who had been "taken with the farye" by washing it, and its shirt in water from a south running stream. The two people who had collected this water had been enjoined to do so without speaking to each other during their journey.[54]

Secondly, the parson of Warlingham in Surrey during the sixteenth or seventeenth century made a manuscript collection of medicines and cures that were "taught him by the Fayries." One of these was a treatment for loss of speech: "take wormwood, stamp it, temper it with water, strain it and out a spoonful in the mouth."[55]

---

53 M. Cartwright, 'Collectanea: Argyllshire,' *Folklore*, vol.21, 90.

54 'Fairies, Egyptians and Elders,' Margo Todd, in Grell & Heal, *The Impact of the European Reformation*, 2008, 193; *Denham Tracts*, vol.2, 140.

55 G.L. Gomme, 'Popular Superstitions,' *Gentleman's Magazine*, vol.3, 1884, 155.

So, to conclude, we have tantalising glimpses of a fresh perspective on the faery world. Loss of speech may well be an integral part of that condition called 'faery blast,' being 'taken' by the fairies or what I've also termed 'elf-addled.' We know, for example, that the illness called 'the fairy' on Orkney implied being struck with dumbness. Thomas Cors, who was tried for sorcery in April 1643, diagnosed those who had lost the power of speech and use of a limb as being subject to "the phairie." Silence may equally be something that's imposed or inflicted upon a person who has dealings with the faeries so as to ensure that their privacy is protected. It's finally worth observing that the infliction of dumbness by the faeries could also be seen in communities as an indicator of being blessed by them with healing powers.[56]

FAIRY PARALYSIS

As we have already seen in the previous section, the impact of faery contact can be both physical as well as mental. What's more serious, perhaps, is that the fairies can take revenge upon people by rendering their limbs ineffective. Readers may recall the little Orkney girl who was paralysed by the trows for pestering them at home. In another example, a Shetland man who awoke one night in a house he was visiting, and saw the family's changeling child dancing with a crowd of trows, was so surprised that he blessed himself. This had the predictable effect of scattering the fairy gathering – but not before one of the trow women had touched one of the visitor's big toes – leaving it paralysed for the remainder of his life. Far worse than this, though, people can be rendered completely incapable of movement by the fairies. This is generally inflicted as some sort

---

56 See 'Fairies, Egyptians and Elders,' Margo Todd, in Grell & Heal, *The Impact of the European Reformation*, 2008, 203; Dalyell, *Darker Superstitions*, 539; *Records of Orkney*, folios 57 & 261.

of punishment and can be a short-term measure to remedy a temporary problem – or it may be a long-term state, indicative of a very different state of affairs.[57]

A lazy, drunken farm labourer from the Cotswold area of England sneaked away from the harvest work in the fields to drink beer in the sun. He chose a small mound with a hawthorn growing on top as comfortable spot and settled down to relax. However, a crowd of small green beings soon appeared in front of him. Despite his fear, he found he was completely unable to move. After a while, they disappeared and he recovered the use of his limbs; to recover from his nasty fright, he needed a drink, but found that all the beer in his flask had also disappeared.

It seems very clear that the shirker had chosen a fairy hill to laze upon. The incident might simply be a case of the faeries stealing alcohol because they fancied their own binge, but it seems more likely that this is an incident of a trespass being punished and – at the same time – a human being chastened for infringing the fairies' moral code. Whilst the story doesn't say it explicitly, I reckon we may infer that the shock was such that the man rarely drank afterwards.[58]

Incursion upon the fairies' reserved places seems constantly to be the cause of cases of paralysis. A farmer of Ffridd Uchaf was returning from Beddgelert fair in Snowdonia when he came across a company of fairies dancing. He concealed himself and, whilst he lay in hiding watching them, he fell asleep. As he slumbered, the *tylwyth teg* bound him so tightly that he could not move, after which they covered him over with a veil of gossamer, so that nobody would see him in case he cried out for help. As the man did not return home, his family made a thorough search for him, but in vain. Fortunately, about the same time the next night the fairies returned and freed him and, a little while

---

57 'Manners, Traditions & Superstitions of the Shetlanders,' *Fraser's Magazine,* vol.34, 486.
58 Briggs, *Cotswolds,* 81.

later, he awoke after sleeping a whole night and a day. He had no idea where he was, and wandered about on the slopes of the Gader and near the Gors Fawr until he heard a cock crow, when he finally realised that he was less than a quarter of a mile from his home. This case is comparable to the story of 'Miser on the Gump at St Just.' An old man set out one moonlit night to Woon Gumpus, near St Just, where he had heard that the fairies assembled and where he thought he might be able to steal some fairy treasure. The whole fairy court emerged from under the ground for a feast and the man hoped to snatch some of their gold and silver plates. He was so preoccupied with the precious metals that he neglected to notice that he had been surrounded by spriggans. They threw hundreds of tiny ropes around him and pulled him to the ground, where he was pinched and stung by the entire fairy multitude. At dawn they vanished, leaving him bound with cobwebs, lying on the open moor.[59]

These last cases involve the faeries tying up their victims. More often, they render them immobile in their bodies. A man who unwittingly stumbled upon a fairy market on the Blackdown Hills in Somerset was mishandled by the assembled multitude. He tried to ride through the mass of fairies gathered around the numerous stalls and was "crowded and thrust, as when one passes through a throng of people... He found himself in pain and so hastened home; where, being arrived, lameness seized him all on one side, which continued with him as long as he lived, which was for many years..." Although the writer here, Richard Bovet, calls it 'lameness,' it seems apparent that the rider had suffered some sort of paralysis on one side of his body. A miller at Rothsay in Northumberland objected to the local faeries using his mill at night and violently disrupted one of their assemblies; the offender was pursued and lightly touched by one of the outraged company – the man doubled

---

59 Rhys *Celtic Folklore*, 103–104; Jenkyn Thomas, *Welsh Fairy Book*, 'Three Farmers;' Briggs, *Dictionary*, 299–300.

up and was "bow bent and a cripple to his dying day." A man who met a black spectral hound that haunted Rodway Hill in Somerset brushed against the beast – and was left paralysed for the rest of his days. A Welsh butcher who was rash enough to try to slaughter one of the faery cows, known as the *gwartheg y llyn,* was paralysed in the arm that tried to strike the fatal blow. In the Highlands it is said that any man who comes upon a *bean nighe* washing clothes may catch them, and learn his fate if he can sneak up unawares; if, however, he's seen first, he will be paralysed.[60]

The accused witch Alison Pearson, from St Andrews, learned healing powers from the faeries, but only after they had made her extremely ill. She told her accusers that the first time she had been summoned and went with the faeries "she gat a sair straike frae one of them, which took all the poustie [power] frae her and left ane ill-far'd mark on her syde." This was bad enough, but the elves continued to treat her badly. They threatened and scared her, saying they would kill her if she ever spoke of what she'd seen in Elphame; worse still, "at last they took away the power of her haile syde frae her, which made her lye many weeks." In other words, having already disabled one side of Alison's body, they paralysed the other and left her completely unable to move for several months.

Our last example of faery paralysis comes from Torrington in North Devon. One day at the very beginning of June, 1890, a man was working in a wood. At the end of the day, he separated from his companions to collect a tool he had left nearby. On bending down to pick it up, a strange feeling came over him: he was unable to move and he heard pixies laughing. He realised he was at their mercy. When the man had not returned

---

60 *Pandaemonium* 207; J. Hodgson, *History of Northumberland,* Part 2, vol.1, 305; Whistler, 'Local Traditions of the Quantocks,' *Folklore,* vol.19, 44; Rhys *Celtic Folklore,* 145; Campbell, *Superstitions,* 43 – and see my *Beyond Faery,* 2020, c.3.

home by ten o'clock that night, his wife became very alarmed and went out to look for him. She met her husband emerging from the wood, soaked to the skin. He explained he had been held under the pixies' spell for nearly five hours, capable only of crawling along on his hands and knees. It was dark and he had no idea where he was, as a result of which he fell into a stream, which had the effect of breaking the enchantment. The wood was apparently known for pixie-leading, although this is not really the right term for the man's experience, which was much more akin to a paralysis. Comparable to this story is a case from Tindall Fell in Cumbria. A man called Jwony was ambling home drunk when he reached a stream. He realised that he was probably too unsteady on his feet to get across on the steeping stones safely, so he lay down to sleep on the bank. Even so, he rolled into the stream in his sleep and was unable to get out. As he lay there helpless, he saw that a small man dressed in green, and about twelve inches tall, standing on his shoulder; it seemed to Jwony that this small figure had the power to hold him down in the water. Luckily, Jwony's dog Swan ran home to fetch his wife to help and their approach scared off the fairy. Once again, we have an instance of paralysis, although in this case – contrasted to the Devonian one – the running water seems to have precipitated rather than dissipated the fairy influence. Perhaps, too, like our first example from the Cotswolds, there is some disapproval of inebriation expressed in the faery actions.[61]

Several features unite all these cases: an action which somehow incurs the faeries' displeasure and their sanction on the offender, a loss of bodily function which may vary in terms of extent and/or duration. I have called this fairy paralysis; our forebears seem to have called it something else – 'fairy blast.' It was a familiar enough affliction and a variety of remedies were devised over the centuries. For example, on the Hebrides, it was

---

61 *Transactions of the Devonshire Association*, vol.24, 1892, 52; W. Dickinson, *Cumbriana: Fragments of Cumbrian Life*, 1876, 137–38.

believed that laying cold steel upon the paralysed limb would free the person from being 'faery bound.'[62]

BLIGHTED BY THE FAERIES

Roughly speaking, there are two main ways in which the fairies can make humans sick. One I have already discussed, which is to shoot us with arrows (elf-shot), which leave the victim elf-struck (suffering from a stroke). The other is to blast us with an 'ill-wind' – a condition also sometimes called the evil eye.

Faery Blasts

The condition of being blasted was recognised in England, and was often termed 'the Faerie' but it is from Scotland that we have the better records of the illness and its cure. The evidence mainly comes from the trial of women suspected of being 'witches,' although in reality what they had usually been involved in was the folk healing, using herbs, of the sicknesses caused by fairies and witches. For example, Jonet Andersone of Stirling was tried in 1621: using a shirt worn by her patient and an iron knife, she had diagnosed that the sufferer's illness came from "a blast of ill wind" caused by the faeries. She was also confident that she could cure "a waff of ane ill wind."[63]

Janet Boyman was a healer of Cowgate in Edinburgh who claimed to have learned her skills from a faery. She was described as "ane wyss woman that could mend divers seikness and bairnis that are tane away with the faryie men and wemin." In 1572, she told a mother than her child would die after it had received "ane blast of evill wind" from the fairies when they found it in its cradle, unblessed by the mother and therefore unprotected. This blasting would not have happened, she went

---

62 Gordon Cumming, *In the Hebrides*, 1883, 194.
63 *Records of the Privy Council*, 2nd series, vol.8, 345–7.

on to aver to the parents, if "thair had been ane disch quhomillit on the feit of the bairne;" possibly this means a dish or bowl made of cow horn, but the etymology is extremely uncertain. Be that as it may, Boyman claimed to have seen at least twenty other cases of fairy blast, and as such was something of an expert in the subject.[64]

In January 1662 Jonet Morrisone, a folk healer living on the isle of Bute, was tried for witchcraft. Amongst the evidence against her was an incident where she had told a man called McPherson that his daughter was paralysed and unable to speak because of "blasting with the faryes," something she cured with herbs. She had treated at least two others in the same way, one being the child of John Glas, who had been taken by the faeries. Morrisone also said that a devil had told her that the fairies had killed a third child and might kill its father also. She and several other island women had the skills to treat these blastings, a condition which also seems to have been called the "Glaick in children."[65]

Janet Trall of Perth treated a baby that had got "a dint of evil wind" by bathing it with water from a south-flowing well; Jonet Miller of Kirkcudbright also used south flowing water to treat illnesses, amongst which she diagnosed a child struck down with the "ferrie blast."[66]

There were two explanations as to how blasting happened. Healer Catie Watson of Stow explained in 1630 that she could cure people who had been "blasted with the breath of the fairy" at Beltane.[67] Jonet Morrisone, though, explained to her inquisitors the precise differences between 'shooting' and 'blasting.' Her statement is worth reproducing in her own words:

---

64 Witchcraft papers, JC40/1.
65 McPhail, *Highland Papers*, vol.3, 20–28.
66 *Extracts of the Presbytery Book of Strathboyce*, 1843, xi.
67 NAS/ms/CH2/338/1 fol.25.

"Againe being inquired quhat difference was betwix shooting and blasting sayes that quhen they are shott, ther is no recoverie for it, and if the shott be in the heart they died presently, bot if it be not at the heart they will die in a while with it – yet will at last die with it – and that blasting is a whirlwinde that the fayries raises about that persone quhich they intend to wrong and that tho ther were tuentie present yet it will harme none bot him quhom they were set for, quhich may be healed two ways: ether by herbs or by charming and that all that whirlwind gathers in the body till [at] one place; if it be taken in time it is the easier healed and if they gett not meanes they will shirpe [shrivel] away."[68]

Janet Boyman in 1572 expanded a little on this: the purpose of the blasting was, in her opinion, to enable the fairies (the "sillyie wychs" as she called them) to abduct the victim. She saw blasting as part of a longer-term strategy, therefore, rather than as an immediate response to some offence. Boyman's pathology seems to have been supported by Bessie Dunlop from Ayrshire, who diagnosed a baby to have been "tane away with ane evill blast of wind, or elf-grippit." Like others, she treated these conditions with herbs. Dunlop was advised in the herbs to use by her faery guide, the dead soldier called Thom Reid, over and above which, she had her own direct experience of being 'blasted by the faeries.' On one of the first occasions that she was introduced to the fairies by Thom, they had departed in "ane hideous uglie sowche of wind," which left her sick until Reid returned and restored her.[69]

---

68 McPhail, *Highland Papers*, vol.3, 27.
69 Pitcairn, *Ancient Criminal Trials*, vol.1, 49–58.

Other Afflictions

In addition, the fairies could blight and debilitate in a variety of other ways. Overall, medical practitioners recognised that a patient might suffer from being "haunted by fairies" and that she or he might have been "stricken with some ill spirit."[70]. These malign attentions might manifest in various conditions, depending upon the exact causes. People might sicken and fade away, having been shot with elf-arrows; they might display similar but much more sudden symptoms after abduction and – as we've seen – they might fall victim to paralysis.

If a fairy breathed upon a person, they might be covered in huge blisters.[71] A lesser version of these symptoms, the rash called 'hives,' was known in the Scottish Highlands as the fairy-pox or *a' bhreac-sith.*[72]

The fairies are particularly well known for their pinching, and severe and persistent symptoms of this were treated as a condition in its own right. In his attack on the idea of witchcraft, *A Candle in the Dark*, which was written in 1655, Thomas Ady noted that:

> "There are often found in Women with Childe certain spots black and blew, as if they were pinched or beaten, which some ignorant people call Fairy Nips."

Another book of 1672, a satirical attack on Catholics, mentions the stigmata, which one priest does not have although "he may have fairy nips, which are as bad."[73]

In 1671, playwright Henry Carey hinted at a belief that even greater harm may have been suffered by young victims of this condition, for it was known that:

---

70 John Gaule, *Select Cases of Conscience Touching Witches*, 1646, 49
71 Stewart, *Shetland Fireside Tales*, 228.
72 McPhail, Hebrides Folklore, in *Folklore* vol 11, 1900, 44.3
73 Ady, *Candle*, 129 (see too his *Perfect Discovery of Witches*, 1661, 128); *An account given to a Catholic friend of Dr Stillinglfeet's late book*, 13.

"like children, just alive,
Pinched by the fairies, never after thrive."[74]

Enlargement of the spleen was also believed to have been inflicted by vengeful fairies. Thomas Lupton in 1579 made reference to "hardnes of the syde, called the Elfe-cake." Herbalist William Langham in his 1597 book *The Garden of Health* prescribed certain 'simples' to "heale elfe cake and the hardnesses of the side."[75]

In conclusion, I should observe that some cases of fairy blast or paralysis seem to be the result of simple contact with or proximity to fairies and tend to be, as a result, of temporary duration. This kind of condition is well-illustrated by the case of a woman who was visited by 'spirits' at Rye in Sussex in 1607. Susan Snapper was the wife of a sawyer and the faeries first came to her about midnight in the middle of Lent that year. One of her visitors, a woman dressed in green, wanted to take Susan with them and gripped her arm to try to drag her away. She resisted and woke her husband to help her. The faeries promptly vanished, but Susan's arm was 'lame' (numb and useless) for two days afterwards and her husband, who had touched her arm when she had cried out, likewise had a numb hand for a couple of days.

On a later occasion, Susan heard a sound in their attic and, going up, saw a light which immediately disappeared. However, she was instantly "taken in suche sorte as shee could not wagge hande or foote and her speeche was taken from her." She remained helpless like this until her husband came looking for her. Then she recovered the feeling in her limbs, but she was unable to speak again until she had descended downstairs. This paralysis and dumbness might be ascribed to shock, or it might have been inflicted by the fairies to show their power, to punish her for resistance or as a penalty for interference.[76]

---

74 Henry Carey, *The Generous Enemies*, Epilogue.
75 Lupton, *Thousand Notable Things*, VII 182; Langham *Garden* 2.
76 G. Slade Butler, 'The Appearance of Spirits in Sussex,' in *Sussex Archaeological Collections*, vol.14, 1862, 25–34.

Banshee Blights

Finally, we must note that there is a distinct folklore of faery blights in the Scottish Highlands. To begin with, there is the Highland tradition of the "wildly roaming fairy woman." In one respect, she acts rather like a will o' the wisp or a mischievous pixie and leads travellers astray, but she has a far more malign trait. She carries with her nine cow fetters, an initially innocuous sounding item which comprises a hobble made of plaited horse hair with a wooden toggle that is used to keep cows still during milking. With these the fairy woman strikes men and pronounces a charm:

> "I place thee under enchantments and crosses, under the nine shackles of the roaming, wandering fairy dame, that the most stunted and weakliest little calf take off your head, and your ears, and your livelihood, if you rest night or day, where you take your breakfast, that you will not take your dinner, and where you take your dinner, you will not take your supper, till you find out the place I am in, under the four red divisions of the world."

Men struck in this manner are rendered doomed, foolish and helpless; they are entirely in the *bean sith's* power and are obliged to do her bidding, however perilous the task imposed. This state might be akin to the paralysis discussed earlier, or it may be an example of the mental effects of faery contact. Either way, it is a unique feature of Highland faery lore. In fact, it appears that the fetters themselves have some inherent magical power that can be used against – as well as by – fairies. In a story from Morvern, some of the *sith* wanted to steal a cow but had to give up and return empty handed because the dairymaid, after milking it, had struck it with the shackle or cow-spancel (*burach*).[77]

---

77 J.F. Campbell & J.G. McKay, *More West Highland Tales*, 1940, vol.1, 231, 413–417 & 425; Campbell, *Superstitions*, 82 & 132.

The menacing and deadly fairy woman (*bean sith*), though, is common in Scottish folklore. For example, in the far north of Scotland a green woman carrying a 'goblin' child is known to pass from cottage to cottage, bathing her baby in the blood of the youngest infant in each household. Another green woman conveys the small pox around communities. In the West Highlands, a *bean sith* called 'the Dame of the Fine Green Kirtle' is regarded as generally skilled and friendly, but at the same time she has great physical strength and is powerful in the magic arts. She can sometimes bewitch men into endlessly wandering the world, searching for her, or else into doing her bidding.[78]

This dangerous female is sometimes referred to in Gaelic as the "slender woman of the green kirtle," (*bean chaol a chota uaine*). The adjectives that are used to describe her, *caol* and more especially *seang*, can mean slender in the sense of graceful, but they can also imply skinny, lean, gaunt or even starving, possibly denoting a creature who's more skeletal and threatening. For example, the water wraith that haunted the River Conon in Ross-shire was said to be a tall woman in green with a withered face. The Linn of Lynturk was haunted by another green woman who attacked night-time travellers. The hungry look of these beings reminds us of the vampiric tendencies of some *glaistigs*. In this context, various Gaelic prayers and invocations that seek to deflect the bane, contempt or hurt of fairy women may be highly significant.[79]

78 H. Miller, *Scenes & Legends of the North of Scotland*, 1835, 15; Campbell & McKay, *More West Highland Tales*, vol.1, 355; Campbell, *Popular Tales of the West Highlands*, vol.2, 410–411 & 435; A. Campbell, *Waifs & Strays of Celtic Tradition*, vol.2, 338 & 485.
79 Carmichael, *Carmina Gadelica*, vol.2, 329 and vol.3, 37, 69 & 227; McPherson, *Primitive Beliefs in North East Scotland*, 1929, 63; MacDougall & Calder, *Folk Tales and Fairylore*, 259.

KILLING AT A DISTANCE

"They are fairies; he that speaks to them shall die."[80]

Worryingly, for those interested in faery lore, it seems that faery-kind possess the ability to kill humans without necessarily intending to do so and/or without taking any direct or violent measures against them. I will give various examples of this.

In the Highlands, the *loireag* is a fairy female who has been described as a "small mite of womanhood who does not belong to this world but to the world thither." Her primary concern is with cloth making, but she will steal milk from cattle in the fields and, despite her benign description, is capable of simply scaring people to death if they meet her.[81]

Sometimes, merely being in the faery's presence can be fatal. For instance, a woman in Ross-shire one time came across a *bean nighe* (a faery washerwoman) cleaning clothes in a stream. The *bean* offered to row the woman across the nearby loch, help she accepted gratefully, but she was dead within a year. The *bean nighe* is seen as predicting imminent deaths, but here she acts as the medium as well. In a similar Highland account, a girl met a green lady beside a loch. The colour of the woman's clothes would immediately have raised alarm, yet all that happened was that she asked the girl if the water there was deep. Soon after this faery encounter, the girl was dead. In accounts from elsewhere in Ross-shire, the belief in the fatal effects of faery conversation is underlined. One witness described how there are two types of little people – land and sea faeries. If the latter speak to you, you will soon drown; if the former address you, you know you will be short-lived.[82]

Faery touch might be fatal too. A Shetland man was returning from fishing one night when he saw a trow hillock standing

---

80 Falstaff, *The Merry Wives of Windsor,* Act 5, scene 5.
81 Carmichael, *Carmina Gadelica,* vol.2, 300.
82 *www.tobarandualchais.co.uk,* July 1960.

open and dancing taking place within. He was invited in and had a great time. On departing, one of the trows clapped the fisherman on the shoulder in a friendly way. The spot turned sore and, within a short time, he was dead.[83]

Most curious of all, however, are several stories of Scottish faery beings that reveal a macabre and alarming power to kill remotely, without needing to touch or even to be in the presence of the victim. The first concerns a *bauchan* or *bogan* that haunted a human farm at Lochaber. There was a powerful love-hate relationship between the faery and the tenant farmer and they often fought. One time, after the farmer had had a confrontation with the *bauchan,* he realised that he'd lost his best handkerchief. He searched for it and came across the *bauchan* sitting, rubbing the cloth on a rough stone. Challenged, the *bauchan* remarked "It's well you've come, Callum: I'd have been your death if I'd rubbed a hole in this."[84]

This curious incident is not entirely isolated. Glenmoriston, at the southern end of Loch Ness, was haunted by a hag called the *Cailleach a' Craich.* Her habit was to waylay solitary travellers, pull of their caps, and then dance on these on the highway until a hole had been worn through – which would prove fatal to the owner.[85]

A third case concerns a man called Donald who was celebrating his wedding to his neighbour's daughter. The party ran out of whisky so Donald went to get some more. Returning home, he was crossing a bridge when a small woman appeared to him in a flash of light. She pulled off his scarf or neckerchief and then proceeded to wash this in the river below, cackling to herself. Donald returned to the party but started to feel weak. He was advised that what the woman was doing was rubbing a

---

83 *www.tobarandualchais.co.uk,* 1955.
84 J.F. Campbell, *Popular Tales of the West Highlands,* vol.2, 103.
85 A. Macdonald, 'Scraps of Unpublished Poetry & Folklore from Glenmoriston,' *Transactions of the Gaelic Society of Inverness,* vol.21, 1896, 34.

hole in his heart and that he had to retrieve his scarf from her, although this had to be done without violence. He recovered the item, but he struck the faery with a stick whilst doing so, which cursed him then to nightly fights with her for the next seven years.[86]

Why is it that damaging an item of clothing might kill its former wearer? The reasoning seems to be that something of the person's spirit or life force is transferred to the garment and can be accessed and destroyed through it. The same sort of thinking lies behind one of the folk healing techniques that was often viewed as 'sorcery' in the Scottish witch trials of the sixteenth and seventeenth centuries. As I've mentioned before, a lot of these purported witches (individuals who had often acquired their healing knowledge from the faes) were able to diagnose and then treat illnesses and afflictions using people's shirts and blouses. These were often washed in south-flowing streams and put on again, the sickness or evil influence being washed away and the charmed water having a beneficial effect on the patient.

---

86 *www.tobarandualchais.co.uk*, January 1979.

CHAPTER FIVE

Defending Against *Them*

Our relationship with the fairies is complex, an amalgam of fear, caution, fascination and wonder. The primary emotions, nevertheless, are defensive. The fairies can do us harm; they are unpredictable, often invisible and yet omnipresent. In response, human culture has become saturated with precautions against the injury that fairies can inflict. They may simply tease or annoy us, but in the worst instances they can make us physically – even mortally – ill.

Fairy pranks are numerous. The 'unseelie court' in Scotland, the wicked fairies, might enter a house at night whilst the occupants slept and shave off a man's hair and beard, just for the amusement. On Shetland, sea trows would enter homes when the humans were out at work, disordering the contents or putting out the fire.[1]

A perpetual source of entertainment (to them) and annoyance and peril (to us) was the fairy habit of leading us astray at night. People might be pixy-led on Exmoor in revenge for some perceived offence (which might be as little as seeing the pixies by chance) or they might make the fog come down on Dartmoor just to laugh at the effect on travellers. Fortunately, turning a sock, or a pocket or a coat would be enough to dispel their enchantment.[2]

---

1 Rogers, *Social Life in Scotland,* 256; *Old Lore Miscellany,* vol.4, 1910, 3.
2 Snell, *Exmoor,* 255; Tozer, *Devonshire,* 76 & 81; Northcote, 'Devonshire Folklore,' *Folklore,* vol.11, 1900, 212; see my *British Pixies,* 2021, c.8.

The fairies could also cause long-term sickness, as we've already seen. The conditions caused go by different names across Britain, terms which change from era to era and place to place. In medieval and early modern times, people might be said to be 'haunted with fairies' or to have suffered the 'ferrie blast' and many charms and rituals were devised to ward off harm.[3]

TREATING THE TROWS

As a short overview to the sections that follow, I will briefly survey the measures employed against the assaults of trows on Orkney and Shetland.

On July 16th 1640 Katharine Craigie was tried for witchcraft on Orkney as a result of the diagnoses and cures she had offered to sick people. One dying man had been advised by Craigie that he was afflicted by some sort of faery, either "ane hill spirit, a kirk spirit or a water spirit." These were evidently trows, as is indicated by the testimony of another suspected witch, Katharine Jonesdochter, in 1616. She avowed that she had seen "trowis ryse out of the kirkyeard of Hildiswick and Holiecross Kirk of Eschenes, and that she saw them on the hill callit Greinfall at monie sundry tymes…" In the case in question, Craigie had found that a kirk spirit was involved and had treated the man by washing him. Another of her patients was afflicted by a hill spirit; another suspected witch, Katharine Caray, had determined in 1617 that a person had been made ill by "ane for the sey" (a sea spirit or sea trow).[4] The same beliefs persisted well into more modern times. Even in the late nineteenth century, therefore, a prayer or grace was recorded on Skye that was recited to protect the old and young, wives and children, sheep and cattle, from 'the power and dominion of the fairies.'[5]

---

3 See, for example, George Giffard, *A Dialogue against Witches*, 1603, 35, or the case of Scottish witch Jonnet Miller (1658).

4 Dalyell, *Darker Superstitions*, 509.

5 McPhail, 'Hebrides Folklore', *Folklore*, vol.11, 1900, 443; Stewart, *Shetland*

Life was hedged about with barriers to fairy incursion. From time to time, of course, they would penetrate those defences – or catch a person who had been unwary – and they then had the opportunity to inflict harm. After such an attack, healing would inevitably be required. On Shetland, there were known 'trowie doctors' who were able to "tell awa' the trows" – in other words, drive away the fairy influence with spells. A variety of spells and charms were deployed. One involved taking water from the breaking surf, heating three stones from the beach and dropping them in the water, turning three times in each direction and then passing the stones through the smoke of the fire three times.

The exact treatment recommended depended, of course, upon the diagnosis. The trows could cause several illnesses. One, called 'feckless heart wear,' manifested itself through the sufferer losing their appetite and wasting away. The cure was a ritual known as 'carstin' (or) runnin' da hert.' The patient sat in a tub by the fire with a bowl of water balanced on his or her head. Some lead was melted and was then poured through the holes in the ends of two crossed keys into the water in the bowl, whilst invoking God's grace. The lumps of lead that formed in the water were carefully examined and the one that most resembled a heart was tied in a rag that was hung on the sick person's chest for three months. During this time, small doses of the water in which the casting took place would be drunk by the patient.

Other known diseases were 'ill winds' blown in people's faces by the trows, which caused languor, stupor and loss of appetite, and 'dead man's nip,' a skin complaint involving discoloured spots somewhere on the body. Rubbing on earth from a graveyard and brushing the mark with a Bible were recommended. Comparable illnesses would affect livestock, too, such as 'elf-shot' and 'taken by fairies' and similar treatments

---

Fireside Tales, 228; Macgregor, 'Ancient Mythology & Modern Superstition', *Celtic Magazine*, vol.3, 1878, 52.

were applied – for example, dissolving salt in water and pouring it in the animals' ears and throat, or giving them water to drink in which a silver coin had been placed.[6]

SACRIFICES TO FAIRIES

One strategy to avert or terminate animosity is to appease the faes. It's not at all unusual for people to make regular offerings to fairies and, on certain occasions, to offer major sacrifices to them. The precise difference between 'offering' and 'sacrifice' is hard to determine. In both cases, property is thrown or given away by the donor; the main distinction may be the manner of its donation – destruction by slaughter or burning perhaps being more properly termed a sacrificial act. Interestingly, though, the ballad *Tam Lin* refers to those passing the fairy hill of Carterhaugh leaving a *wad* (that is, a 'wed' or pledge) for the fairies. This makes the 'gift' sound much more like a transaction or guarantee, a payment for protection from the faeries. What's more, in this case what's demanded from young women is "Either their gold rings, or green mantles, Or else their maidenhead." The faes demand a high price for a person to be free of their malign attentions and, as we saw in chapter two, sexual exploitation may never be far away.

It was the habit in the Scottish Highlands and islands to make regular offerings of milk to the *gruagach* and *glaistig* who often looked after the cattle on farms and in communities. Small quantities were poured out on special stones, perhaps after every milking or at certain times in the farming year. At Pier o' Wall, Westray, on Orkney, stand two burial mounds called Wilkie's Knolls. Milk used to be poured daily into a hole on top of one of these. If this was neglected, the resident spirit called Wilkie would steal clothes, haunt homes and bring down plague

---

6 Nicolson, *Shetland Folklore,* 79 & 168; *Old Lore Miscellany,* vol.9, 1933, 18.

on the cattle. A case from East Lothian brings out part of the thinking behind these offerings. Tried before a church court at Humbie, in 1649, Agnes Gourlay was accused of pouring milk down the drain for the fairies; her justification was "God betuch us to [God preserve us]; they are under the yird [earth] that have as much need of it as they that are above the yird." In fact, at least as recently as the 1950s milk was still put out overnight for the pixies on one Dartmoor farm.[7]

At Alnwick in Northumberland, an old woman in early Victorian times is recorded to have told one folklorist that she regularly put out "a loake [a small amount] of meal and a pat of butter" for the fairies. She then explained that she got a "double return" from them for her mark of respect. As suggested just now, it can often be hard to determine whether these 'gifts' of food were provided out of sympathy and neighbourly kindness (as with Agnes Gourlay), out of fear of a supernatural power or as a kind of bargain, as appears to have been the case in Alnwick.[8]

Fear is plainly the motivation in the next example. In Aberdeenshire, there are two hills topped by wells at which travellers must make a small sacrifice to the *bean-sith* (fairy woman) of the hills. The customary offering is a barley meal cake, marked with a circle on one side, which is placed beside the well. Neglecting this can have dire (and swift) consequences: for instance, one woman failed to leave a cake at the well and fell dead at a cairn only a short distance away. At Loch Maree in the Scottish Highlands, appeasement was plainly the motive. A terrible lake monster called Mourie inhabited the lake, to which bulls were sacrificed on August 25th each year.[9]

---

7 *New Statistical Account*, vol.14, 275 – Kilmuir, Inverness; Wentz, *Fairy Faith*, 177; Dalyell, *Darker Superstitions*, 193.
8 *Denham Tracts*, vol.2, 143.
9 W. Gregor, 'Notes on Beltane Cakes,' *Folklore*, vol.6, 1895, 5; Wentz, *Fairy Faith*, 437; Spence, *British Fairy Origins*, 176.

Many other offerings are more transactional. On Shetland, local people sacrificed ale or pins and coins to the water horse called *shoopiltee* to ensure good catches at sea. At Halloween, the people of Lewis used to attend a church ceremony that included pouring ale into the sea in the hope that the sea spirit 'shony' (*seonaidh)* would guarantee a good supply of seaweed in the year ahead; so too on the remote isle of St Kilda, where shells, pebbles, rags, pins, nails and coins were thrown into the waves. All round Scotland, in fact, meat, drink and bread would be offered up. On Orkney the custom was that the first fish caught on a hook when out line-fishing would be thrown back to ensure that the rest of the catch from that trip would be good.

A very similar practice was known on the Isle of Man. The islanders used to sacrifice rum to the buggane of Kione Dhoo headland, the liquor being poured into the sea by fishing boats from Port St Mary as they passed the promontory on their way to the Kinsale and Lerwick fishing grounds. Rum was occasionally thrown from the top of the cliff as well, with the words "Take that, evil spirit (or monster)!". This dedication resembles that which accompanied the Manx practice of throwing a fish to the mermen when at sea: *"Gow shen, dooinney varrey!"* ('Take that, sea people.')

Further south, in the Lincolnshire Fens, the habit used to be to offer the first fruits of the harvest, as well as a share of any bread, beer and milk, to the local spirits called the 'Strangers,' 'the Tiddy Ones' or the 'Green Coaties.' People knew that if these offerings were neglected, their crops would fail and livestock would die.

The success of many regular household tasks can be guaranteed by making sure of faery good will. For instance, on the Isle of Man, the faeries will help with the baking so long as a piece of the dough is stuck to the kitchen wall for them. If such an offering isn't made, the baker will face problems. On Shetland the practice was to sprinkle every corner of a house with milk when butter was to be churned. On mainland Scotland, just as with the milk offerings mentioned earlier, some of the wort from any household brew of ale would be poured out at the 'brownie stone' to ensure a good fermentation.

Faery aid – or good will – may be invoked in emergencies too. One Dartmoor sheep farmer's flock was plagued by disease; he concluded that the only remedy was to go to the top of a nearby tor and to slaughter a sheep for the pixies – a move which proved to be justified as it promptly alleviated the problem. At Crawford Muir on Shetland in the 1770s a tenant was reported to have sacrificed a black lamb to the sea trows so as to reinforce curses he was placing upon his enemies.

Lastly, and most strikingly, in 1859 on the Isle of Man archaeologists opened a barrow near Tynwald Hill and excavated the prehistoric remains within. After they had left, in order to atone to the little people for this desecration of their site, a local farmer sacrificed and burned a heifer on the tumulus. This dedication to the spirits of the place is especially striking but the act itself seems to have been fairly common on the island. Professor John Rhys records an early nineteenth century instance of a live sheep being burned on May Day as a sacrifice.[10]

These final examples are particularly notable because they so much resemble Old Testament sacrifices of lambs and the like. Whilst the annual killing of a bull at Loch Maree may be regarded as a more obvious *quid pro quo* with the faery beast – giving it an animal to eat in order to try to avert uncontrolled predation – the examples from Man, Dartmoor and Shetland have much more pronounced magical or religious and propitiatory aspects. The faery presence is evidently conceived of as a 'higher power' to be appeased – or even to be worshipped.

---

10 *Manchester Times*, April 2nd, 1881, 4; Rhys, *Celtic Folklore*, vol.1, 306–308.

OBJECTS AS CHARMS

A study of the folklore records reveals that a wide range of objects, many of them extremely ordinary, have been found to be efficacious as charms that ward off or repel faery harm. They fall into several broad categories, although most of them are natural materials.

Minerals

A number of commonly occurring rocks and such like substances seem to dispel the fairy presence. Iron is by far the most famous of these, being effective in any shape – whether a knife, a horse shoe, a pin or needle, tongs, keys or the bolt of a door. As well as repelling the faes, iron can be used to rescue people from dances in faery rings. One unusual, but effective, use of iron is in the form of ploughshares. In a number of Scottish cases, wives and children kidnapped by the faeries have been recovered from the faery hill by means of the father or husband ploughing around the knoll, in one case doing so three times in a clockwise direction. This remedy presumably combines several potent threats: not least is the steel of the coulter, but in addition there are the magical number and direction as well as the simple fact of the risk of physical damage to the faery dwelling.[11]

An almost unique story from Bronnant in Cardiganshire suggests that the faery aversion to iron can be transferred to those who have prolonged contact with them. In perfectly standard fashion, a girl was lost in a faery ring and was rescued from the dance after a year and a day; what distinguishes the tale is that she warned her rescuers that none should ever strike her with iron. Subsequently, this happened by accident and she

---

11 *Bye Gones,* May 13th 1885, 216 & May 9th 1888, 95; *www.tobarandualchais. co.uk,* Nov. 23rd 1969 & May 19th 1982; Rhys, *Celtic Folklore,* 200; Campbell, *Superstitions,* 46–47 & 84.

vanished forever. Very similar is the experience of a shepherd from Afon Fach Blaen y Cae, a stream that runs into the Dwyfach on the Lleyn peninsula. One day, whilst looking after his flock, he came across a group of the little people who were about to dance. They detained him and he married one of their number. He was told that he would live happily with them as long as he would never afterwards touch any instrument of iron. For years the family lived very happily. One day, however, he unknowingly touched something made of iron, with the consequence that both the wife and the children immediately disappeared. This reverses the usual Welsh theme of an accidental contact with iron driving off a faery wife and is again suggestive of the effect of extended association with 'them.'[12]

A second very unusual piece of Welsh evidence states that – against all expectations – some faeries may become very attached to individual humans and will accompany them constantly, becoming a burden for the chosen 'friend.' The only way to sever this attachment was to pelt the unwanted companion with rusty iron (something that will also prove very effective with changelings).[13]

Despite the widely recognised efficacy of iron and steel, and its ready availability, several other equally potent materials may be enumerated. A hot coal, thrown in a vat of brewing ale, will prevent the faeries spoiling it; live coals carried by travellers will prevent them being misled or abducted during their journey. If faeries are seen in the act of trying to steal a child, water in which an ember had been doused – or burning turves – may be thrown at them.[14]

Amber beads sewn into a child's clothes will prevent its abduction.[15] Salt will certainly drive off the fairies, whether

---

12 Rhys, *Celtic Folklore*, 249 & 108.
13 Rhys, *Celtic Folklore*, 250 & 231.
14 Rogers, *Social Life in Scotland*, 1886, vol.3, 263; Campbell, *Superstitions*, 37 & 47.
15 *County Folklore*, vol.7, 113.

scattered around or put into food stuffs that you don't want stolen.[16] In the Highlands, calves' ears were smeared with tar just before May Day so as to protect them against theft.[17]

The last, rather well-known natural object in this category is the so-called adder stone, a naturally holed rock or pebble that could be worn around the neck to protect an individual or might be hung over a byre or stable to safeguard livestock, both from taking and from riding at night by the fairies. For example, in Hadleigh in Suffolk, hanging such 'hag stones' over stable doors was recommended a sure way of protecting the horses from fairies at night. When not in use, these stones were often kept safe in iron boxes which stopped the fairies trying to interfere with them. The antiquarian Edward Lhuyd, visiting Scotland in 1699, recorded that these 'self-bored' stones were also known as snake buttons, cock-knee stones, toad stones, snail stones and mole stones.[18]

Plants

It is pretty well known that sprigs of rowan (also called mountain ash) repel faeries.[19] If a piece of rowan is cut between two Beltane days, it will act as a charm to protect men, women children, horses and cattle against the fairies.[20] At Tongland, near Kirkcudbright in Fife, tying rowan or service tree branches to the stakes of cattle would protect them from fairies and witches.[21]

16 *Mannin*, no.1, 1913, 'Folklore Notes.'
17 Campbell, *Popular Tales*, 63.
18 G.L. Gomme, 'Popular Superstitions,' *Gentleman's Magazine Library*, vol.III, 1884, 123; Edward Lhuyd, letter to Martin Lister, Dec. 15th 1699; G.F. Black, *Scottish Charms & Amulets*, 1894, 462–70.
19 *Yn Lioar Manninagh*, vol.4, 35; in Lincolnshire, rowan was laid on the churn for the same effect – M. Peacock, 'Notes on Prof. Rhys' Manx Folklore,' *Folklore*, vol.2, 1891, 510
20 G. Sinclair, *Satan's Invisible World Discovered*, 1685, 126–127.
21 *Old Statistical Account of Scotland*, vol.9, 1793, 328.

The rowan tree is merely the most familiar example, but a wide range of herbs, weeds and shrubs are equally repulsive to the faes. For example, fresh nettles, if laid on a milk churn, will stop them hindering the churning (according to Manx belief). In this connection, see Edward Guilpin's play *Skialaetheia* (1598) in which a character says "I applaud myself, for nettle stinging thus this fayery elfe." The stings of nettles may be as unpleasant to faery kind as to humans, but with other plants some less obvious quality is effective. Vervain and dill can both dispel evil influences, as can milkwort and mugwort. Other handy herbs are mistletoe, nightshade, rue, groundsel root, ash-tree sap, yarrow, heather and bindweed.[22] In Wales, it was said that a four-leaved clover (combined, apparently, with nine grains of wheat) helped you to penetrate their glamour and to see the fairies – which would certainly enable you to avoid them if need be.[23] In the Braemar district of the Scottish Highlands, the fairies could be barred from entering homes down the chimney at night by the simple means of placing a piece of fir timber across the mouth of the chimney.[24]

On the Hebrides, St John's Wort and pearl wort both granted a general protection to cattle and people. The pearlwort, called *mothan* in Gaelic, would prevent the fairies taking the *toraidh* or substance of human foodstuffs; it could guard cattle against elf-shot (see earlier) and it could defend against the substitution of changelings. To safeguard cattle, for instance, three tufts of the herb were to be picked on a Sunday in the name of the Holy Trinity and were then concealed, wrapped in a cloth, in the milking parlour or byre. In one account, a baby had just been born at a house when a *loireag*, a hairy little being, was seen at the door. A voice called out to it "Bring him out!" but the faery

---

22 *Mona Miscellany*, 2nd series, vol.2, 1873, 194; *Aberdare Times*, July 11th 1891, 2; *Llangollen Advertiser*, Nov. 9th 1888, 4; *Cardiff Times*, October 8th, 1904, 1.
23 *Cardiff Times*, Dec. 26th 1874, 3; *Rhondda Leader*, Sept. 17th 1904, 7.
24 E. Taylor; *The Braemar Highlands*, 325.

replied that she couldn't because the milk of a cow that had eaten *mothan* was in the child's stomach. Another story tells how a girl who used to tend her family's cattle on the moor began to come home late in the evening because she had become friendly with the local *sith* folk, who would invite her into their knoll. The parents feared that this was building up to an abduction, so they made her wear sprigs of *mothan* tucked under her belt – a simple measure which stooped the *sith* taking her.[25]

As we saw earlier, oatmeal has a special protective power. On Skye, oat cakes were said to have a protect against the *sith*. Likewise, on Tiree, oats in the pockets could guard travellers and outdoor workers against faery perils. In the region around Ben Nevis and Glencoe, a bannock hung over the threshold of a house would safeguard a mother and her new-born child within; the smoke generated by holding an oatcake close to a fire will repel all kinds of malign spirits. Quite whether this protection derives from the oats themselves or the fact that they have been processed and very possibly salted in less certain. In some unfathomable way, it seems, these facts must be related to a story from Arisay, in which some girls tending cows saw a knoll open and heard music coming forth. Impelled by curiosity and drawn by the music, they went to look in, but were scared off by a woman who emerged clapping her hands and shouting "*cruas choirce,*" which means "hardness of oats."[26]

In county Durham, an elder branch was said to guard against both witches and fairies – even though in other places (the Isle of Man for example) the fairies were said to dwell in elder trees; elder sprigs could also be carried to ward off the faes – and even to strike them.[27] Also on the island of Man, a willow

---

25 Mackenzie, *Gaelic Incantations, Charms & Blessings of the Hebrides,* 1895, 29; *www.tobarandualchais.co.uk,* October 4th 1976.

26 *www.tobarandualchais.co.uk,* November 23rd 1969 & May 1954; A. Stewart, *Twixt Ben Nevis & Glencoe,* 1885, 261.

27 W. Brockie, *Legends & Superstitions of the County of Durham,* 1886, 114 & 119.

cross would protect against *bugganes* and *fynoderees*, but how much efficacy derived from the wood and how much from the religious significance of the shape, it's very hard to judge (see later for religious items).[28]

In Michael Drayton's poem *Nymphidia*, the fairy Nymphidia uses a range of herbs to protect the fairy queen against Puck. These include fern-seed, mistletoe kernels, nightshade straws and the juice of rue, gathered from beneath a yew tree. Part of her spell making also involves crawling under and jumping over an arched briar, both ends of which had set down roots:

> "Then thrice under a Bryer doth creepe,
> Which at both ends was rooted deepe,
> And over it three times shee leepe;
> Her Magicke much avayling:"

The list of herbs given by the poet is reasonably familiar, but the last detail about the bramble bush is especially fascinating. In Cornwall, crawling through a briar arch was recommended as a cure for boils or whooping cough. This detail may also explain, perhaps, a puzzling report from the Isle of Man. A boy from Andreas parish once went out bird-nesting. He passed a large briar bush and his face "slipped all to one side." The local people were sure that this had been done by the little people. The record of the incident that we have does not expand upon *why* they thought this to be the case, but perhaps Drayton offers a clue as to what might have been going on. There would seem to be some faery power in the bush – something that, by his proximity or some other perceived disrespect – the boy had violated.[29]

Lastly, it's very interesting to note an aspect of supernatural belief from the Scottish Highlands. Herbs like *mothan* had

---

28 Dora Broome, *Fairy Tales from the Isle of Man*, 1963, 95.
29 *Choice Notes & Queries, Folklore*, 88 & 217; *Yn Lioar Manninagh*, vol.2, 194.

inherent properties that repelled faery malice, but for them to be most effective they had to be gathered "*gun iarraidh*" ('without searching' – literally, 'without asking'). Another authority on Highland folklore confirms this, recording that another plant used to protect both people and their livestock from fairy blight, St John's Wort, had to be picked whilst repeating the following charm:

> "Unsearched for and unsought (*gun sireadh, gun iarraidh*),
> For luck of sheep I pluck thee."[30]

Animal Products

An odd variety of animal parts and by-products could prove revolting to fairies – some understandable, some more surprising.

Drawing blood was believed to drive off the faeries on both Orkney and Shetland. This might, possibly, have some connection with the belief in some parts of Britain that the faes were a bloodless race – although this is not a universal conception and there are definitely folk tales in which faery blood is shed. Somewhat similar, perhaps, is the Highland belief that spitting in a child's face when it yawns will act as a safeguard against faery interference.[31]

On the Isle of Man, two bones were found to have powerful effect. These were the *crosh bollan,* which is the upper part of the palate of the wrass fish, and the so-called *Thor's Hammer,* which is in fact from a sheep's mouth and which prevents fairy leading. This same charm was known in northern England too.[32]

---

30 Mackenzie, *Gaelic Incantations, Charms & Blessings of the Hebrides,* 1895, 29.

31 *Old Lore Miscellany, Orkney & Shetland,* vol.1, 1907, 162; Spence, *British Fairy Origins,* 92–3 & 163.

32 *Mannin,* no.3, 1913, 2; Dora Broome, *Fairy Tales from the Isle of Man,* 1963, 76–79; *Denham Tracts,* 58.

The reasons for the efficacy of the Manx fishbones are hard to define, although shape may be a significant factor – the name of Thor's Hammer perhaps indicating an inherited belief from Norse religion. Some animal products, however, are far easier to explain. They repel faes because they are noisome. Near Stirling, in mid Scotland, it was recorded in 1795 that new born calves would be forced to eat a little dung as this would protect both witches and elves harming or stealing them. In the Highlands, a woman and her newly delivered baby could be safeguarded from abduction by putting an old shoe on the fire – the resulting stench repelled the faes.[33]

On the Scottish mainland, a strip of sheep skin, *caisean-uchd*, that had been removed from the carcase without a knife, would be burned and inhaled to protect the household for the coming year. Beating a cow's hide and burning dried skin from a cow's neck were equally effective charms for driving away the *sith* folk on New Year's Eve.[34]

One of the most effective animal by-products was urine, or *maistir*. At Shewbost on the Hebrides the fairy cattle, the *crodh mara*, used to come ashore to graze and the local people were able to catch them and add them to their own stock by the simple measure of sprinkling *maistir* across their path back to the sea. Furthermore, mermaids – just like the faeries – also have an aversion to the substance. Sprinkled between the mermaid and the sea, she would not be able to cross and could then be captured as a 'wife' (or perhaps sex-slave). Even so, these charms were only effective so long as the urine was renewed daily. In one account, the person responsible one day forgot to sprinkle 'fresh' *maistir* and, as soon as she detected it, the captive mermaid escaped, calling the cows by name to follow her.[35]

---

33 *Old Statistical Accounts of Scotland,* vol.16, 1795, Killearn; Campbell, *Superstitions,* 36.
34 MacGregor, *Peat Fire Flame,* 42–43.
35 MacPhail, *Folklore from the Hebrides,* II, 384.

A sprinkling of *maistir* around a house will protect the resident household from the faes. Accordingly, it was renewed regularly in the Scottish Highlands, being applied on the last evening of every quarter of the year. *Maistir* is especially helpful just after a baby has been born, when both nursing mother and child need to be protected against the risk of abduction. Perhaps on the same basis, carrying the mother over the drain from the cow shed is reckoned to be equally effective. In fact, *maistir* can be a general protective against bad luck. On the Isle of Man, for example, ploughs would be washed with the substance before they were taken out to the fields for the annual ploughing; from Cornwall too, there comes a reference to throwing 'stale water' over the ploughs to keep the little people away – a more discrete reference to the same practice, I believe. In Ross-shire, all new born babies were bathed in urine (or *uisge-or* – 'golden water) to prevent the fairies stealing them.[36]

Changelings could be driven away, forcing the faeries to return their infant captive, by exposing them to a range of unpleasant conditions, of which the mildest involved *maistir*. A suspected changeling could be laid on top of the pot in which the liquid was being stored and, because of the stench, this might alone be enough to expel it.

Cloth Items

It's quite well-known that red threads are effective against fairies, for example tied around a child's throat or on a cradle to protect them from taking or woven into the hair of a cow's tail to prevent the faeries stealing its milk. If you wanted to double your protection, securing a spring of rowan to someone or something with a red thread was recommended.[37]

---

36 Campbell, *Superstitions*, 49; *Choice Notes & Queries – Folklore*, 1859, 147; 'Folklore Survivals from Ross-shire,' *Folklore* vol.14, 381.

37 *Byegones*, May 2nd 1905, 302; *New Statistical Accounts of Scotland*, vol.15, 1845, 142; Campbell, *Superstitions*, 36–37.

A burning rag carried round a woman in childbirth three times would stop the fairies taking her and her new born baby, it was said on Orkney and Shetland. It's also reported that, when the trows smelled the smoke from the rag, they would express their displeasure in a rhyme:

"Wig wag, jig jag,
Ill healt so weel
Thu wes sained
Wi' a linen rag."

To be fair, though, the smell of the smouldering material was probably the really effective part of this ceremony – for comparison, burning peats were also carried around farms on Shetland at Yule to ward off the trows and burned sheep's hide was used elsewhere as we've seen. The combination of the stinking smoke plus the flame (recall the lit coals earlier) appear to have been what discouraged the trows.[38]

Religious Items & Imagery

Linked possibly to the erroneous belief that fairies are fallen angels or emissaries of the devil and, as such, innately antithetical to all aspects of Christian religion, items such as bibles, psalm and prayer books were constantly regarded as sure remedies against faery threat. Even a few pages torn from a holy book could work, it was said in Scotland: it had been found that an open bible could be especially potent, if carried around the person or place to be blessed and protected. Alternatively, you can blow across the bible at the person to be protected. An example of this type of protection comes from Cumberland. A man returning late from Bewcastle market was pulled from his horse and dragged across the county to a fairy hill. Had he not

---

38 *Old Lore Miscellany, Orkney & Shetland,* vol.1, 1907, 162 & vol.7, 1914, 28.

had a page from the Bible in his pocket, he would have been forced inside. Carving a cross on a baby's cradle could protect and even placing items in a cross shape, whether iron tools or just straws, was also found to be highly efficacious.[39]

ACTIONS AS CHARMS

The last section described how a variety of objects and substances function as powerful charms against fairies. In this section, I look at how some actions and words can have a like effect.

Some of the effective actions will be familiar to readers from wider magical practice. For example, drawing a circle around yourself – especially if an iron or steel point is used to do this – will guard an individual.[40] Making the sign of the Christian cross is widely believed to be effective in the same manner as, of course, are Christian prayers or the invocation of holy names, typically the trinity, but also those of individual saints. For example, on the Shetland island of Yell any girl who set out from home on an errand or a journey would be blessed by her family to protect her from trows on the way.[41]

On South Uist, babies that had to be left alone in their cradles by their mothers because they had to go out would be protected by their father's shirt thrown across them, with the sign of the cross and with a verse:

---

39 H. Bulkeley, 'Some Cumberland Superstitions,' *Transactions of the Cumbrian & Westmoreland Antiquarian Society,* vol.8, 1886, 227; J Macdiarmid, 'Fragments of Breadalbane Folklore,' *Transactions of the Gaelic Society of Inverness,* vol.26, 1905, 38; *www.tobarandualchais.co.uk,* May 19th 1982; Campbell, *Superstitions,* 36–7; J. Maxwell Wood, *Witchcraft & Superstitious Record,* 146.
40 Catton, *History & Description of the Shetland Islands,* 1838, 116.
41 *www.tobarandualchais.co.uk,* December 18th 1972.

> "When Halloween comes be there, be there,
> Fairies and devils will be plentiful, plentiful;
> Happy fairies will be marching in the sky,
> Stealing wives and children, and children."[42]

A mother's wedding dress could have the same protective qualities.[43]

Another secular charm, used on the island of Eriskey to protect cattle left grazing on the hills, was to say "Closed be every hole; clear be each knowe; and may the hardship of Columbkille be upon you until you come home."[44]

Some actions are less easily explicable. For example, there is a very peculiar (and frustratingly incomplete) account recorded in Charles Rogers *Social Life in Scotland*. He describes how the fairies had abducted the wife of the miller of Menstrie but he then reports how, when riddling meal one day at the door of his barn, the husband stood in a particular stance or posture that had the effect of breaking the spell and recovering his spouse. He's said to have stood on one leg, like a hen in wet weather, though it's not at all clear why this had the effect it did.[45]

Another bizarre ritual treatment comes from Shetland, where calved cows could be protected from the trows by drawing a cat along and across their bodies. This performance appears to be effective either because it marks the beast in a cross shape or creates a magic circle around them (although it has to be confessed that this explanation leaves the precise role of the cat unresolved).[46]

Most typically, it was forms of words that were effective against the faes (over and above simply blessing yourself and

---

42 *www.tobarandualchais.co.uk*, September 1966.
43 Campbell, *Superstitions*, 37.
44 Hull, *Folklore of the British Isles*, 153.
45 Rogers, 1886, vol.3, 258.
46 *New Statistical Account of Scotland*, vol.15, 1845, 142 (Sandsthing & Aithsting).

calling on God). Volume III of Alexander Carmichael's *Carmina Gadelica* (Gaelic Songs) contains a range of spoken charms that offer protection against fairies. Many of these are addressed to individual saints, including Brigit, Mary, Michael, Peter, James, John and Columba. Their assistance is sought either against generalised perils or to help with specific threats. One example, a general invocation to God, seeks "Blessing from the hurt of the silent women, wanton women, fairy women and world women." I take this list to comprise different ways of labelling the same individuals, given that *sith* can denote both 'fairy' and 'peaceful/silent,' and considering too the notable wantonness of such females as the *leannan sith*. Another blessing invokes "God between me and every faery" (*Dia eadar mi's gach siodha*).[47]

On waking in the morning, you can pray (as we've already seen) to "Ward off the bane of the fairy women" (these *bean sith* were plainly seen as a persistent danger, as several prayers are concerned with them); the fairies of the knolls (*siodach nan cnoc*) are also mentioned. The *sith* folk as a whole were seen as especially threatening on Thursdays (when a blessing could be intoned against them) and at the time of death, when a person might pray to be shielded against the evil of the faeries (*bho arrais nan sidh*).

More precisely identified risks include faery arrows or darts (which are mentioned in several prayers) and the fairy host or sluagh. St Michael's aid was requested against the host and fairies more generally: "*cha dean sluagh... cha dean siodh.*" As well as people, household items and equipment might be protected, as in this blessing for a loom against *gruagachs* and faery women: "*Bho gach gruagach is ban-sith.*"[48]

---

47 J. Maxwell Wood, *Witchcraft & Superstitious Record,* 153; Carmichael, *Carmina,* vol.I, 9, 31, 175, 305 & 327; vol.II, 59 & 353; vol.III, 37, 69, 109, 133, 161, 182, 223, 227 & 391.
48 Carmichael, *Carmina,* vol.3, 223 & vol.1, 305.

William Mackenzie also recorded *Gaelic Incantations* that he heard on the Hebrides before 1895. He came across a charm against injuries to the spleen and liver by the *sith* folk as well as more comprehensive charms guarding against the 'nine slender faeries' (*'s air naoi bean seang sithe*) and their arrows, or against a more pervasive malign fairy influence:

"We repudiate their evil tricks,
(May) their back be to us,
May their face be from us,
Through merit of the passion and death of our saviour."

The *Mona Miscellany* of 1873 recorded a very similar incantation from the Isle of Man that was to be said at night to protect a home from incursions by the Little People during the hours of darkness:

"The peace of God and the peace of man,
The peace of God on Columb Killey,
On each window and each door,
And on every hole admitting moonlight,
And on the place of my rest
And the peace of God on myself."[49]

Directly comparable to this is a grace that was recorded from a resident of Skye, Farquhar Beaton, during the 1840s, when he was one hundred years old. Nightly he prayed for protection for the old and young, wives and children, sheep and cattle against the 'power and dominion of the faeries' (*o churnhach agus cheannas nan sithichean*). Some might perhaps question the credulity of people saying such prayers, but as Beaton himself said – "My two eyes beheld them; my two ears heard them"

---

49 Mackenzie, *Gaelic Incantations, Charms & Blessings of the Hebrides,* 1895, 51–52; *Mona Miscellany,* 2nd series, vol.21, 1873, 195.

(*Mo dhu shuil fein a chunnaic iad; mod ha chluas fein a chual iad.*) He'd seen the threats posed by the *sith* and he was taking no chances...[50]

One thing to bear in mind with all of these verbal charms, I am sure, is the need to repeat them in the exact form in which they have been formulated. The Isle of Man supplies a very good example of the consequences of failing to do this, which is to be found in Dora Broome's *Fairy Tales of the Isle of Man*. A man wanted to find a fynoderee to help cure his sickly cow and his wife told him a charm to repeat to lure one out of a tree and into his power:

> "Fynoderee, fynoderee
> Come down, for I can see."

The being would then follow the husband anywhere, but she warned him to cross himself three times immediately after saying the words, for fear of *butcheragh* (witchcraft, or bad magic). Of course, the husband forgot the gesture to go with the charm, and bad luck followed: his cow recovered from its illness, but it disappeared along with the fynoderee – and all the other animals and birds living on the farm.[51]

Finally, and not at all to be imitated, there is a strange piece of advice from Scotland. It was believed that the faeries would be unable to abduct a child if she or he had a patch of burnt skin on their body. If a child had fortuitously had an accident, this might safeguard them, but it is very clearly not to be recommended as a precaution.[52]

---

50 A. Macgregor, 'Ancient Mythology & Modern Superstitions,' in *Celtic Magazine*, vol.3, 1878, 52; Macgregor, *Highland Superstitions*, 1901, 16.
51 Dora Broome, *Fairy Tales from the Isle of Man*, 1963, c.4.
52 *www.tobarandualchais.co.uk*, March 20th 1953.

TREATING FAIRY BLIGHTS

As I described in the previous chapter, the faeries can inflict illness upon both children and adults. The symptoms of this vary, but one tell-tale sign is for the patient falling into a steady decline, which is the result of the faeries abstracting the individual's substance. Losing the power of speech (as already seen) as well as the loss of use of a limb, were also recognised in the past as being indicative of being struck with "the phairie." In 1593 George Giffard recorded a case of a London man who claimed that his neighbour's wife was much troubled because she was "haunted with a Fairy."[53]

A range of cures and ceremonies were devised for those afflicted in this manner by faeries. John Milton gives us an interesting glimpse of this type of medicine in his poem, *Comus*. He describes how the nymph Sabrina:

> "... oft at Eve,
> Visits the herds along the twilight meadowes,
> Helping all urchin blasts, and ill luck signes
> That the shrewd medling Elfe delights to make,
> Which she with pretious viold liquors heals."

Here, of course, we have the intriguing contradiction of a faery curing faery-inflicted harms – but this seems to be a regular feature of fairy healing skills.[54]

Another indication of faery pharmaceutical or medicinal skill comes from William Percy's play of 1603, *The Faery Pastorall*. The faes inform a sickly human that "we will bestowe on you a

---

53 Dalyell, *Darker Superstitions of Scotland*, 538–539, citing Grant, *Parish of Suddie* MS, for year 1732 & trial of Thomas Cors, April 6th 1643 in *Records of Orkney*, folio 261; Giffard, *A Dialogue Concerning Witches & Witchcrafts*, 1593, 4.

54 Milton, *Comus*, 1634, lines 843–7.

well mesurde Peck of our Faery comfits to comfort your carsye stomach with them."[55]

There are a number of key ingredients or procedures regularly found in the cures, as are discussed in the following paragraphs.

Herbs

One medieval source advised parents whose children had been taken by the faeries to "take the roote of gladden and make poudre thereof, and geve the sike both in his metes and in his drynkis and he schal be hool withinne ix days and ix nyghtis, or be deed, for certeyn." 'Gladden' is the iris or orris, the roots of which dried can be anti-inflammatory and will remove toxins from the body; fresh, the whole plant is highly poisonous, perhaps explaining the rather fatalistic tone of the text.[56]

William Langham, writing in 1597, endorsed similar remedies. Children 'haunted' by faeries and goblins should have a bag containing peony seeds and root hung around their necks, he advised, whilst a linen cloth soaked in oil of bay was recommended by him as an excellent treatment for fairy pinches. You may recall from the first chapter that children in Northumberland were protected from abduction in a faery ring by wearing peony roots and seeds in bags round their necks. Peonies can be eaten as vegetables and their roots are tonic and antispasmodic, being used in the past to treat epilepsy. Infused in mead, the seeds were said to help prevent nightmares, possibly indicating why Langham might have recommended the plant.[57]

In fact, a range of faery-related illnesses would be treated with herbs. For such maladies as "ane evill blast of wind" or

---

55 *Faery Pastorall,* Act V, scene 4.

56 *Promptorium Parvulorum,* c.1440: footnote to entry for 'elfe,' from Sloane MS 73 f.125.

57 Langham, *The Garden of Health,* 1597; *Denham Tracts,* vol.2, 140.

being "elf-grippit" (having a fairy attack or seizure) the Scottish witch suspect Bessie Dunlop had offered a variety of cures. She would mix assorted herbs together to feed to sick cattle; illnesses in people might be cured by ointments or by powders (which were presumably ingested); during her examination in court she added that if the patient "sweated out" the treatment, they would not recover. Just like Bessie, Jonet Morrisone from the isle of Bute used herbs to heal a little girl who'd been 'blasted with the faryes.' Rather like Bessie, too, she told the court at her trial in 1662 that treatment in time should guarantee recovery, but if she was consulted too late, the patient might still "shirpe" (shrivel or wither) away.[58]

Herbs seemed to do more than cure illness in livestock and people, though. Janet Wier of Edinburgh told her trial in April 1670 that her fairy helper, a woman who interceded on Janet's behalf with the fairy queen, also gave her a piece of tree or herb root which allowed her to "doe what she should desyre." Elsewhere in Scotland flax (the blue-eyed one of the fairy women' *gorm-shuileach na mna sith*) was used both as a medicine and to protect people against attacks by the elves and the *sluagh*.

Water from Wells & Rivers

As I have described previously, faery kind have an ambivalent relationship to wells, sometimes inhabiting them, sometimes avoiding them, sometimes giving their waters healing properties. In Wales, wells would be protected from the fairies by circling them with stones painted white; however, the water from some springs was reputed to keep the fairies at bay – for example, St Leonards Well at Sheep's Tor on Dartmoor.[59]

---

58 Pitcairn, *Ancient Criminal Trials*, vol.1, 49–58; McPhail, *Highland Papers*, vol.3, 20–28.
59 *Cardiff Times*, Marcg 9th 1907, 1; *The Standard*, July 24th 1873, 4.

Water can have magical properties in faery cures. Stein Maltman of Stirling told his 1628 trial that he made several different uses of water in his cures. He boiled elf-shot in water from a south-flowing stream and either had a patient drink it or bathe in it; in another case Maltman had a man bathe himself in such a stream having first diagnosed his patient's illness by reciting charms over one of the man's shirts.[60]

South-flowing streams were also regarded as especially efficacious by Janet Trall from Perth. She sought to cure a baby who'd had a blast of 'evil wind' by washing it in water collected in silence from a south-running spring. After the child was bathed, the water was carried back to the well together with the child's shirt in the bucket and both were cast into the water. Silence in carrying out these rituals appears to have been a very significant element in the curative process, as already discussed in the cases of Catie Watson and Jennet Pereson. Margaret Hormscleugh, also from Perth, likewise used south-running water in her cures. It had to be fetched from and returned to the spring in silence, and the person carrying the jugful of water had to ensure that its mouth faced north whilst it was transported. Marioun Grant of Aberdeen, tried for sorcery in 1597, also prescribed the use of south-running water fetched in silence.[61]

Rituals and Other Items

Our last category of curative techniques involves a mixture of odd materials that were considered to have medicinal effect. Medieval cures included prayers, such as one recommended for where a child was "elfe-y-take." The parent was advised to "sey

---

60 Alaric Hall, 'Folk-healing, Fairies and Witchcraft: The Trial of Stein Maltman, Stirling 1628,' *Studia Celtica Fennica* III (2006) 10–25.
61 *Extracts of the Presbytery Book of Strathboyce*, 1843, xi; *Denham Tracts*, vol.2, 140; 'Fairies, Egyptians and Elders,' Margo Todd, in Grell & Heal, *The Impact of the European Reformation*, 2008, 192; *Spalding Club Miscellany*, vol.1, 170.

iii tymes thys verse: *Beata mater munere* [Holy Mother help me].
In the worchyppe of God and of our Ladie, sey iii pater noster
and iii aveys and a crede and he scal be hole."[62]

The aforementioned Stein Maltman rubbed some of his
patients with elf-shot; over others he waved a drawn sword, on
the basis that the naked iron would scare the malignant fairies
away; finally, he advised some of those who consulted him to
return to the spots where they felt they had picked up their
infections, there to pray for healing.[63]

Even something as simple as noise might deal with a faery
haunting. A woman in Suffolk was troubled by a 'pharisee' in
bed. She scared it away by hitting her warming pan and then
hung a holed adder-stone over the bed so as to keep the faery at
a distance.[64]

A Shetland boy had been made ill by the trows. His parents
were advised to tether a calf to his bed and offer it to the 'grey
folk.' The next morning, the boy was well and the calf had died.
This appears to be a sort of sacrifice, exchanging one desirable
life for another.[65]

Of all the cures prescribed by local healers, those performed
by Katharine Jonesdochter of Shetland are amongst the
strangest. She had been seduced by a faery man who came to
her when she was only a "young lass" and still living with her
mother. Over the intervening forty years he visited her regularly
and had given her two items to use in curing. One was a 'sea
nut,' presumably a coconut that had washed ashore, and the
other was a 'cleik,' a large iron hook. She was able to cure
cows that had stopped giving milk with the hook whilst the nut
protected them from the danger of trow assaults. Combined, the

62 *Promptorium Parvulorum,* c.1440: footnote to entry for 'elfe.'
63 Alaric Hall, 'Folk-healing, Fairies and Witchcraft: The Trial of Stein
   Maltman, Stirling 1628,' *Studia Celtica Fennica* III (2006) 10–25.
64 G.L. Gomme, 'Popular Superstitions,' *Gentleman's Magazine Library,* vol.III,
   1884, 123.
65 *www.tobarandualchais.co.uk,* September 15th 1975.

two items enabled her to transfer sickness from one person to another.[66]

Also on both Shetland and Orkney, illness could be diagnosed and treated through the bizarre ceremony of 'casting the heart.' It was believed that consumptive illnesses were the result of faeries (or witches) causing the victim's heart or other organs to weaken and waste away. To confirm the exact nature of the problem, molten lead was poured into a bowl of water held by the sufferer. The metal was run into the water through the loop at the end of a key or the handle of some scissors or shears. This was repeated until a lump resembling the heart or lungs was made; this showed how and where the patient was afflicted and demonstrated that the spell had now been broken. The sick person then wore the lead effigy around the neck until they made their full recovery.[67]

Timing

Just as important as the right herbs and water could be the timing of any attempt at healing. This is brought most clearly in the case of Scottish healer Jonet Boyman, who told one man that she wouldn't be able to assist him because it had passed Halloween, which is when "the guid nychtbouris rysis that day and had mair acquaintance with that day nor anie uther." In other words, the Good Folk were abroad in the mortal world and more accessible to us at this point in the calendar; having missed it, it would be very hard for Boyman to contact them.

James Knarstoun of Kirkbuster on Orkney divined the cause of a girl's illness using the process of 'casting the heart' just described; as part of this ceremony he specified that the water involved had to be collected from a particular local well and that this could only be done between midnight and cockcrow.

---

66 *Court Book of Shetland 1615–1629*, 1991, 39–40.
67 *New Statistical Account of Scotland*, vol.15, 143.

What's more, this entire technique was something which had to be performed at the correct phase of the moon.[68]

The acquisition and application of fairy knowledge seems to be intimately entwined with the fairies' calendar. Katharine Jonesdochter of Shetland received her healing powers from a spirit she called the Bowman, who for forty years had visited her either at Halloween or on Holy Cross day in September. Marion Or of Dundonald acquired her healing skills by riding with the Fair Folk at the festival of Beltane. The same was claimed two years later (1604) by Jonat Hunter, of the same town; she also claimed to have received from the faeries the ability to "tell many things –" amongst them being the identity of thieves.[69]

Summary

As the preceding paragraphs will make clear, over the centuries people have amassed an impressive armoury of tools and techniques for combatting the worst assaults of faery-kind. The vast majority of these, fortunately, involve commonly available and inexpensive ingredients, making them accessible to all – regardless of income or circumstances. Nevertheless, the deployment of these defences may well require skill and care: the proper words and rituals must very often accompany the use of the materials to assure the best outcomes.

---

68 Dalyell, *Darker Superstitions*, 511.
69 *Court Book of Shetland 1615–1629*, 1991, 39–40; 'Fairies, Egyptians and Elders,' Margo Todd, in Grell & Heal, *The Impact of the European Reformation*, 2008, 193–195.

Conclusion

The increasing tendency of contemporary society is to see faeries as winged, friendly and helpful creatures, as beings whose sole purpose appears to be the maintenance of the natural world and the amelioration of human life. Like mermaids, they have become fit figures for little girls to dress as at parties.

This image of Faery is almost wholly at odds with the evidence of nearly two millennia of folk experience in Britain. Until the last few generations, people lived in uneasy accommodation with our 'Good Neighbours,' always cautious and often fearful of them. We forget our forebears' hard-won knowledge at our peril. As this book has endeavoured to show, the faes have seldom been our friends and allies. Their assistance is mercurial and may easily be lost; their powers are considerable and can cause us great damage and loss if they choose to wield them against us. This book has sought to set out the 'darker side' of faerie simply to give an honest and balanced assessment of faery nature. To forget or underestimate this can prove perilous.

Lightning Source UK Ltd.
Milton Keynes UK
UKHW021117201021
392517UK00004B/37